Clover Series

# READING LEADER

## ROBERT HICKLING

KINSEIDO

**Kinseido Publishing Co., Ltd.**

3-21 Kanda Jimbo-cho, Chiyoda-ku,
Tokyo 101-0051, Japan

First published 2024 by Kinseido Publishing Co., Ltd.

Design        Nampoosha Co., Ltd.
Illustrations   Toru Igarashi

Photos
p.14   © Navapon Plodprong | Dreamstime.com
p.20   © Siraphol | Dreamstime.com
p.26   © Pindiyath100 | Dreamstime.com
p.38   © Iakov Filimonov | Dreamstime.com
p.50   © Jjfarq | Dreamstime.com
p.62   © Fabio Diena | Dreamstime.com
p.74   © Antonello Marangi | Dreamstime.com
p.80   © Aleksey Popov | Dreamstime.com
p.86   © Anna Krivitskaia | Dreamstime.com
p.92   © TOKUSHIMARU Inc.

 音声ファイル無料ダウンロード

https://www.kinsei-do.co.jp/download/4188

この教科書で DL 00 の表示がある箇所の音声は、上記 URL または QR コードにて無料でダウンロードできます。自習用音声としてご活用ください。

▶ PC からのダウンロードをお勧めします。スマートフォンなどでダウンロードされる場合は、**ダウンロード前に「解凍アプリ」をインストール**してください。
▶ URL は、**検索ボックスではなくアドレスバー（URL 表示欄）に入力**してください。
▶ お使いのネットワーク環境によっては、ダウンロードできない場合があります。

CD 00　左記の表示がある箇所の音声は、教室用 CD（Class Audio CD）に収録されています。

# はしがき

*Reading Leader* は段階的に学習できるように構成されたリーディング中心の教科書です。文法項目や語彙を徐々に導入し、後ろのユニットで再利用することで、見慣れない文法や語彙に圧倒されることなく、英語が苦手な学生でも無理なく英文に取り組むことができます。また、大学生に身近な話題から知的好奇心をくすぐる逸話まで幅広いトピックにより、楽しく英文を読み進め、読解力を伸ばすことができます。

本書は1ユニット6ページの構成で、全15ユニットから成ります。各ユニットには共通のトピックについて書かれた2つのリーディング・パッセージと簡潔な文法説明が含まれています。また、各ユニットの最後にはパッセージのトピックに関連する語彙・フレーズを楽しく学べる活動が用意されています。

ユニットの構成は以下の通りです。

## Reading Starter

80〜90語程度の短めのパッセージを読み、話の流れに合わせて4つのイラストを並べかえます。この活動は、文脈を視覚的にとらえることで英文の内容理解を深めるのに役立ちます。また、英文の音声を聞くことで、読解力のみならずリスニング力を高めることもできます。(10分)

## Grammar Review

各ユニットで学習する文法項目を、簡潔な例文とともに図表を用いてわかりやすく説明しています。(10〜15分)

## Grammar Check-Up

A Reading Starterのパッセージをもう一度読み、Grammar Reviewで学習した文法項目を含む箇所を探します。この活動は、学習した文法項目が、文脈の中でどのように使われているかを確認し、文法項目についての理解を深めることを目的としています。(5分)

B 学習した文法項目の理解を確認するための練習問題(8問)です。空所に入る語句を3つの選択肢から選び英文を完成させた後、音声を聞いて答えを確認します。(10分)

## Reading Helper

このセクションには2つの目的があります。

● 学習した文法項目の理解を確かなものにするための練習問題(4問)です。日本語の意味に合うように、英文の空所に入る語句を選択肢から選び記入します。必要に応じて語句の形を変えて記入するユニットもあります。

● 次ページのReading Challengerのパッセージに登場する重要語句を予習します。マーカーが引かれた重要語句の意味や文中での使われ方を、日本語訳を参照しながら確認し理解することで、Reading Challengerへの挑戦を助けます。(10分)

## Reading Challenger

A Reading Starterと同じトピックについて書かれた170語程度の長めのパッセージを読みながら、空所に入る語句を2つの選択肢から選びます(6問)。設問は文法と語彙の両方を扱っており、文脈に沿って判断することが求められます。その後で、英文の音声を聞いて答えを確認します。この活動では、積極的に英文に取り組みながら、文法と語彙の両方の理解度を確認し、リスニングを通して答えを確認することで、内容の理解を深めることができます。(15分)

B 4つに分けられた1、2文の英文を正しい順番に並べかえ、パッセージのサマリーを完成させます。英文の論理の流れをとらえる力を養成します。(5分)

C パッセージの内容の理解を問う問題(4問)です。パッセージの内容について書かれた英文の空所に入る語句を2つの選択肢から選び、英文を完成させます。(5分)

# Useful Words & Phrases

A リーディング・パッセージのトピックに関連するフレーズを学びます(6問)。空所に入る語句を選択肢から選んでフレーズを完成させた後、音声を聞いて答えを確認します。(5分)

B Aで完成させたフレーズとイラストをマッチさせます(6問)。フレーズを視覚的なイメージと結び付けることで、表現の定着を図ります。(2~3分)

C 50~60語程度の短いパラグラフを読み、空所に入る語句を選択肢から選び記入します(7問)。必要に応じて語句の形を変えて記入するユニットもあります。Aで学んだ語彙やフレーズがいくつか含まれているので、文脈の中でそれらがどのように使われているかを確認することができます。(5分)

最後に、本書の制作にあたり、金星堂の皆様から多くのご助言、ご支援をいただきました。この場をお借りして御礼申し上げます。

Robert Hickling

# 本書はCheckLink対応テキストです
チェックリンク

CheckLink のアイコンが表示されている設問は、CheckLinkに対応しています。
CheckLinkを使用しなくても従来通りの授業ができますが、特色をご理解いただき、
授業活性化のためにぜひご活用ください。

## CheckLinkの特色について

大掛かりで複雑な従来のe-learningシステムとは異なり、CheckLinkのシステムの大きな特色として次の3点が挙げられます。

❶ これまで行われてきた教科書を使った授業展開に大幅な変化を加えることなく、
専門的な知識なしにデジタル学習環境を導入することができる。

❷ PC教室やCALL教室といった最新の機器が導入された教室に限定されることなく、
普通教室を使用した授業でもデジタル学習環境を導入することができる。

❸ 授業中での使用に特化し、教師・学習者双方のモチベーション・集中力をアップさせ、
授業自体を活性化することができる。

### 教科書を使用した授業に「デジタル学習環境」を導入できる

本システムでは、学習者は教科書のCheckLinkのアイコンが表示されている設問にPCやスマートフォン、アプリからインターネットを通して解答します。そして教師は、授業中にリアルタイムで解答結果を把握し、正解率などに応じて有効な解説を行うことができるようになっています。教科書自体は従来と何ら変わりはありません。解答の手段として CheckLinkを使用しない場合でも、従来通りの教科書として使用して授業を行うことも、もちろん可能です。

### 教室環境を選ばない

従来の多機能な e-learning教材のように学習者側の画面に多くの機能を持たせることはせず、「解答する」ことに機能を特化しました。PCだけでなく、一部タブレット端末やスマートフォン、アプリからの解答も可能です。したがって、PC教室やCALL教室といった大掛かりな教室は必要としません。普通教室でもCheckLinkを用いた授業が可能です。教師はPCだけでなく、一部タブレット端末やスマートフォンからも解答結果の確認をすることができます。

### 授業を活性化するための支援システム

本システムは予習や復習のツールとしてではなく、授業中に活用されることで真価を発揮する仕組みになっています。 CheckLinkというデジタル学習環境を通じ、教師と学習者双方が授業中に解答状況などの様々な情報を共有することで、学習者はやる気を持って解答し、教師は解答状況に応じて効果的な解説を行う、という好循環を生み出します。 CheckLinkは、普段の授業をより活力のあるものへと変えていきます。

上記3つの大きな特色以外にも、掲示板などの授業中に活用できる機能を用意しています。
従来通りの教科書としても使用はできますが、ぜひ CheckLink の機能をご理解いただき、
普段の授業をより活性化されたものにしていくためにご活用ください。

# CheckLinkの使い方

CheckLinkは、PCや一部のタブレット端末、スマートフォン、アプリを用いて、この教科書にある  CheckLink のアイコン表示のある設問に解答するシステムです。

- 初めてCheckLinkを使う場合、以下の要領で「**学習者登録**」と「**教科書登録**」を行います。
- 一度登録を済ませれば、あとは毎回「**ログイン画面**」から入るだけです。CheckLinkを使う教科書が増えたときだけ、改めて「**教科書登録**」を行ってください。

登録はCheckLink
学習者用アプリが
便利です。

ダウンロードは
こちらから▶

▶CheckLink URL
**https://checklink.kinsei-do.
co.jp/student/**

## 学習者登録（PC ／タブレット／スマートフォンの場合）

① 上記URLにアクセスすると、右のページが表示されます。**❶学校名**を入力し、**❷「ログイン画面へ」**を選択してください。
PCの場合は**❸「PC用はこちら」**を選択して、PC用ページを表示します。同様に**❹学校名**を入力し、**❺「ログイン画面へ」**を選択してください。

② ログイン画面が表示されたら**❶「初めての方はこちら」**を選択し、「学習者登録」画面に入ります。

PC画面

③ 自分の**❶学籍番号、氏名、メールアドレス**（学校のメールなどPCメールを推奨）を入力し、次に**❷任意のパスワード**を8桁以上20桁未満（半角英数字）で入力します。なお、学籍番号はパスワードとして使用することはできません。
「パスワード確認」は、**❷**で入力したパスワードと同じものを入力します。
最後に**❸「登録」**ボタンを選択して、登録は完了です。次回からは、「**ログイン画面**」から学籍番号とパスワードを入力してログインしてください。

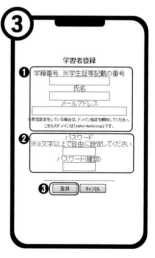

# 教科書登録

**①** ログイン後、メニュー画面から「**教科書登録**」を選び（PCの場合はその後「**新規登録**」ボタンを選択）、「**教科書登録**」画面を開きます。

**②** 教科書と受講する授業を登録します。
教科書の最終ページにある、**教科書固有番号**のシールをはがし、**❶印字された16桁の数字とアルファベットを入力**します。

**③** 授業を担当される先生から連絡された**❷11桁の授業ID**を入力します。

**④** 最後に**❸**「**登録**」ボタンを選択して登録は完了です。

**⑤** 実際に使用する際は「**教科書一覧**」（PCの場合は「**教科書選択画面**」）の該当する教科書名を選択すると、「**問題解答**」の画面が表示されます。

# 問題解答

**①** 問題は教科書を見ながら解答します。この教科書の CheckLink のアイコン表示のある設問に解答できます。

**②** 問題が表示されたら選択肢を選びます。

**③** 表示されている問題に解答した後、**❶**「**解答**」ボタンを選択すると、解答が登録されます。

# ● CheckLink推奨環境

## ＰＣ

**推奨 OS**
　　Windows 7, 10 以降
　　MacOS X 以降

**推奨ブラウザ**
　　Internet Explorer 8.0以上
　　Firefox 40.0以上
　　Google Chrome 50以上
　　Safari

## 携帯電話・スマートフォン

3G以降の携帯電話(docomo, au, softbank)
iPhone、iPad(iOS 9〜)
Android OSスマートフォン、タブレット

●最新の推奨環境についてはウェブサイトをご確認ください。
●上記の推奨環境を満たしている場合でも、機種によってはご利用いただけない場合もあります。
　また、推奨環境は技術動向等により変更される場合があります。

---

公式サイトでは、
CheckLink活用法について
動画で分かりやすく
説明しています

公式ウェブサイト

https://www.kinsei-do.co.jp/checklink/movie

## CheckLink開発

CheckLink は奥田裕司 福岡大学教授、正興 IT ソリューション株式会社、株式会社金星堂
によって共同開発されました。
CheckLink は株式会社金星堂の登録商標です。

---

CheckLinkの使い方に関するお問い合わせ先

# 正興ITソリューション株式会社　CheckLink 係

e-mail　**checklink@seiko-denki.co.jp**

# READING LEADER

## Table of Contents

# Unit 1

# The Cherry Blossom Season in Japan

現在時制

POINT!! ● 主語によって変化するbe動詞の形
● 主語がIとyou以外の単数で、現在時制の一般動詞の形

## Reading Starter

CheckLink　DL 02　CD 02

英文を読み、話の流れに合うようにa〜dの
イラストを並べましょう。

Japanese people love *sakura*, or cherry
blossoms, and foreign visitors do, too.
Every spring, thousands of tourists
come to Japan for *hanami*, or cherry
5　blossom viewing.　They visit famous
cherry blossom viewing spots in parks,
gardens and other beautiful places.　They
also attend cherry blossom festivals,
watch dance performances and eat
10　delicious Japanese food.　*Sakura mochi*,
or sakura rice cakes, are very popular.
Some tourists follow the *sakura zensen*,
or cherry blossom front.　It moves from
south to north across the country.
15　Everyone returns home with wonderful
memories of Japan.

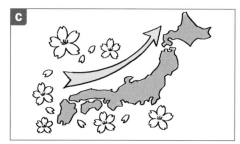

### NOTES

attend「…に出席[参加]する」 follow「…に注目する」
memories「思い出」

1. ☐ ➡ 2. ☐ ➡ 3. ☐ ➡ 4. ☐

11

# Grammar Review

## be 動詞の現在形

### ▶ 形と語順

| 主語 | 肯定文 | 否定文 | 疑問文 |
|---|---|---|---|
| I | I am [I'm] … | I am not [I'm not] … | Am I …? |
| you / we / they* | you are [you're] … | we are not [we aren't] … | Are they …? |
| he / she / it** | he is [he's] … | she is not [she isn't] … | Is it …? |

*複数名詞も同様  **単数名詞も同様

### ▶ 使い方と例文

| 名詞の前 | They're pilots. / They aren't pilots. / Are they pilots? |
|---|---|
| 形容詞の前 | I'm late. / I'm not late. / Am I late? |
| 前置詞＋名詞の前 | She's from L.A. / She isn't from L. A. / Is she from L.A.? |

### ▶ 疑問文の答え方

| 肯定文 | Yes, I am. / Yes, you [we, they] are. / Yes, he [she, it] is. |
|---|---|
| 否定文 | No, I'm not. / No, you [we, they] aren't. / No, he [she, it] isn't. |

## 一般動詞の現在形

### ▶ 形と語順

| 主語 | 肯定文 | 否定文 | 疑問文 |
|---|---|---|---|
| I / you / we / they* | I work [study, do, have, go] | I do not [don't] work [study, do, have, go] | Do you work [study, do, have, go] …? |
| he / she / it** | he works [studies, does, has, goes] | he does not [doesn't] work [study, do, have, go] | Does he work [study, do, have, go] …? |

*複数名詞も同様  **単数名詞も同様

### ▶ 使い方と例文

| 現在の状態を説明する | Ken has a car. / Ken doesn't have a car. / Does Ken have a car? |
|---|---|
| 習慣的な動作を説明する | They work at night. / They don't work at night. / Do they work at night? |
| 一般に認められている事実を説明する | Cats like milk. / Birds don't like milk. / Do rabbits like milk? |

### ▶ 疑問文の答え方

| 肯定文 | Yes, I [you, we, they] do. / Yes, he [she, it] does. |
|---|---|
| 否定文 | No, I [you, we, they] don't. / No, he [she, it] doesn't. |

## Grammar Check-Up

**A** もう一度 **Reading Starter** の英文を読み、動詞の現在形に下線を引きましょう。全部で11か所見つけられますか。

**B** (　　　) 内の a ～ c から適切な語句を選び、英文を完成させましょう。その後で音声を聞いて答えを確認しましょう。　⟳CheckLink　🎧 DL 03　◉ CD 03

**1.** Jennifer and I ( **a.** am　**b.** is　**c.** are ) in the same history class.

**2.** Stanley ( **a.** love　**b.** loves　**c.** is love ) computer games.

**3.** Andrew and Kate ( **a.** are　**b.** does　**c.** is ) from England.

**4.** ( **a.** Is　**b.** Do　**c.** Does ) this bus go to the university?

**5.** This ( **a.** isn't　**b.** doesn't　**c.** aren't ) a good movie.

**6.** ( **a.** Does　**b.** Are　**c.** Is ) it hot outside?

**7.** ( **a.** I doesn't　**b.** I don't　**c.** I'm not ) have my textbook today.

**8.** Do you live with your parents? — Yes, ( **a.** I'm　**b.** I am　**c.** I do ).

## Reading Helper

日本語の意味に合うように、下の◻︎から適切な語句を選び、必要に応じて形を変えて英文を完成させましょう（否定文の場合もあります）。マーカーを引いた語句は次ページの **Reading Challenger** に出てくる重要語句です。

| be | be | grow | last | live | love | speak | visit |
|----|----|------|------|------|------|-------|-------|

**1.** Beth often _____ the city museum.  It _____ full of precious paintings.　（ベスはよく市立美術館を訪れます。そこには貴重な絵画がたくさんあります）

**2.** Tulips _____ in spring. However, they don't _____ long—they bloom for only one or two weeks.　（チューリップは春に成長します。しかしそれらは長くもちません―たった1、2週間しか花を咲かせません）

**3.** I always look forward to Mr. Brown's English class.  He _____ slowly.  Also, his tests _____ difficult.　（私はいつもブラウン先生の英語の授業を楽しみにしています。彼はゆっくり話します。それに、彼のテストは難しくありません）

**4.** I _____ this photo.  It reminds me of my trip to Japan with Peter.  He _____ there now with his Japanese wife.　（私はこの写真が大好きです。それを見るとピーターとの日本旅行を思い出します。彼は今、日本人の妻とそこに住んでいます）

**A** (　　　　) 内の a、b から適切な語句を選び、英文を完成させましょう。その後で
音声を聞いて答えを確認しましょう。　　　　　　　 ✪CheckLink　🎧 DL 04　◉ CD 04

Every year, Japanese university students look forward to the cherry blossom
season.  The beautiful blossoms in spring ¹( **a.** are　**b.** were ) a welcome sight after
a long winter of studying and taking exams.

Students often go to parks with their friends and classmates and ²( **a.** have
5　**b.** make ) cherry blossom viewing parties under the beautiful cherry trees.  There,
students relax, talk and eat together, and enjoy the beauty of nature.

In many parts of Japan, the cherry blossom season ³( **a.** has　**b.** is ) in early
April.  This is the beginning of the school year.  For freshmen, ⁴( **a.** it's　**b.** they're )
also the beginning of the next chapter in their lives.  They meet new people, make
10　new friends and learn new things.  The season is a happy and exciting time.

For Japanese students, their four years of college is a time of great growth and
change.  But just as cherry blossoms bloom for only a short period of time, college
life also ⁵( **a.** goes　**b.** returns ) by very quickly.  The blossoms ⁶( **a.** remember
**b.** remind ) students that life is precious.

**◖NOTES◗**

welcome sight「待ち望んだ光景」　chapter「（人生などの）一区切り、章」　just as ...「…と同じように」

**B** 英文の内容に合うようにa〜dを並べかえ、サマリーを完成させましょう。

CheckLink

**a** Cherry blossoms remind Japanese university students that life is very important.

**b** Students enjoy cherry blossom viewing parties with their friends in parks.

**c** After a long winter of studying, Japanese university students find joy in the beautiful cherry blossoms in spring.

**d** In many cases, the cherry blossom season and the new school year happen at the same time. For freshmen, it's an exciting and happy time.

1. ☐ ➡ 2. ☐ ➡ 3. ☐ ➡ 4. ☐

**C** 英文の内容を正しく述べている文になるよう、a、bから適切な語句を選びましょう。

CheckLink

1. Students look forward to ( a. exams    b. the cherry blossom season ) every year.

2. Freshmen usually feel ( a. excited    b. shy ) at the beginning of the school year.

3. Time passes ( a. quickly    b. smoothly ) for college students.

4. Many ( a. changes    b. problems ) happen during the students' years in college.

# Useful Words & Phrases

**A** 右の ▮▮▮ から適切な語句を選びフレーズを完成させましょう。その後で音声を聞いて答えを確認しましょう。

🎧 DL 05　◎ CD 05

1. ..................................... to a cherry blossom viewing party
2. ..................................... a boxed lunch
3. ..................................... a plastic sheet on the ground
4. ..................................... at the cherry blossoms
5. ..................................... the trash
6. ..................................... a food stall vendor

| |
|---|
| clean up |
| eat |
| gaze |
| go |
| pay |
| spread |

**B** a～f のイラストに合うフレーズを **A** の 1～6 から選び（　　）に書きましょう。

a. (　　)　　　　b. (　　)　　　　c. (　　)

d. (　　)　　　　e. (　　)　　　　f. (　　)

**C** 下の ▮▮▮ から適切な語句を選び英文を完成させましょう。その後で音声を聞いて答えを確認しましょう。

🎧 DL 06　◎ CD 06

| arrive | find | get | go | have | spread | wait |
|--------|------|-----|-----|------|--------|------|

One day every spring, Ken $^1$................ up very early and $^2$................ to the park. He $^3$................ a nice spot under a cherry tree and $^4$................ a plastic sheet on the ground. Then he $^5$................ for his friends. A few hours later, his friends $^6$................ with boxed lunches and drinks, and they $^7$................ a cherry blossom viewing party.

# Unit 2

# Travel Pleasures

## 代名詞

POINT!!
● 代名詞の役割
● 文中の働きによって変化する代名詞の形

  **Reading Starter**

CheckLink    DL 07    CD 07

英文を読み、話の流れに合うようにa〜dの
イラストを並べましょう。

People visit other countries for various
reasons.  Some go for sightseeing.  They
visit famous places and learn about the
history and culture of those locations.

5 Others relax and enjoy nature at beaches
or mountain resorts.  Many students go
on homestays.  There, they learn about
the lifestyles and customs of their host
families.  The host families also gain

10 an understanding of their homestay
students' ways of life.  Some people travel
to other countries for shopping.  They
visit shops and markets, looking for
interesting items to take back home with

15 them.

(NOTES)

sightseeing「観光」  customs「習慣」
ways of life「生活様式」

1. ☐ ➡ 2. ☐ ➡ 3. ☐ ➡ 4. ☐

17

代名詞は前に出てきた名詞の代わりに使われます。同じ言葉を繰り返さないことで、文章をコンパクトにわかりやすくすることができます。

Ed is in a band.  Ed plays the drums.

▼

Ed is in a band.  **He** plays the drums.

エドはバンドをしています。彼（エド）はドラムを演奏します。

This isn't Jennifer's new smartphone.  Jennifer's new smartphone is blue.

▼

This isn't Jennifer's new smartphone.  **Hers** is blue.

これはジェニファーの新しいスマホではありません。彼女のもの（ジェニファーの新しいスマホ）は青色です。

Ann and Ann's brother often visit Ann's and Ann's brother's grandparents.

▼                                ▼

Ann and **her** brother often visit **their** grandparents.

アンと彼女の（アンの）お兄さん[弟]はよく彼らの（アンとアンのお兄さん[弟]の）祖父母を訪ねます。

## 代名詞の格変化 | 文章中の働きによって形が変化します。

| 主格<br>「…は、…が」<br>主語になる | 目的格<br>「…を、…に」<br>動詞や前置詞の後ろに<br>来て目的語になる | 所有格<br>「…の」<br>名詞の前に来て<br>所有を表す | 所有代名詞<br>「…のもの」<br>〈所有格＋名詞〉を<br>1語で表す |
|---|---|---|---|
| I<br>**I** drink tea. | me<br>Dogs like **me**. | my<br>This is **my** pen. | mine<br>The car is **mine**. |
| you（単数）<br>**You** drink tea. | you<br>Dogs like **you**. | your<br>This is **your** pen. | yours<br>The car is **yours**. |
| he<br>**He** drinks tea. | him<br>Dogs like **him**. | his<br>This is **his** pen. | his<br>The car is **his**. |
| she<br>**She** drinks tea. | her<br>Dogs like **her**. | her<br>This is **her** pen. | hers<br>The car is **hers**. |
| it<br>**It** drinks tea. | it<br>Dogs like **it**. | its<br>This is **its** pen. | ----- |
| we<br>**We** drink tea. | us<br>Dogs like **us**. | our<br>This is **our** pen. | ours<br>The car is **ours**. |
| you（複数）<br>**You** drink tea. | you<br>Dogs like **you**. | your<br>This is **your** pen. | yours<br>The car is **yours**. |
| they<br>**They** drink tea. | them<br>Dogs like **them**. | their<br>This is **their** pen. | theirs<br>The car is **theirs**. |

## Grammar Check-Up

**A** もう一度**Reading Starter**の英文を読み、代名詞に下線を引きましょう。全部で６か所見つけられますか。

**B** （　　　）内のa〜cから適切な語句を選び、英文を完成させましょう。その後で音声を聞いて答えを確認しましょう。　　CheckLink　　DL 08　　CD 08

**1.** Ken and ( **a.** he　**b.** him　**c.** his ) wife have two dogs.

**2.** Jack and ( **a.** I　**b.** me　**c.** my ) are in the same history class.

**3.** The teacher gives ( **a.** our　**b.** us　**c.** we ) a lot of homework.

**4.** In Hokkaido, ( **a.** it　**b.** its　**c.** it's ) snows a lot in winter.

**5.** This isn't Tim's car. ( **a.** He　**b.** His　**c.** Him ) is red.

**6.** Meg plays sports. ( **a.** She　**b.** Her　**c.** Hers ) favorite sport is tennis.

**7.** Cathy loves parties, but Mark hates ( **a.** their　**b.** it　**c.** them ).

**8.** This steak is delicious! Do you like ( **a.** his　**b.** its　**c.** yours ), Bob?

## Reading Helper

日本語の意味に合うように、下の　　から適切な語句を選び英文を完成させましょう。
マーカーを引いた語句は次ページの**Reading Challenger**に出てくる重要語句です。

| hers | I | it | its | my | theirs | them | us |
|------|---|----|----|----|--------|------|-----|

**1.** Kyoto is ＿＿＿＿＿＿ favorite Japanese city. ＿＿＿＿＿＿ has many beautiful gardens.
（京都は私の一番好きな日本の都市です。そこには美しい庭園がたくさんあります）

**2.** Mrs. Simpson gives ＿＿＿＿＿＿ free art lessons. Painting is a unique talent of ＿＿＿＿＿＿.
（シンプソンさんは私たちに美術の無料レッスンをしてくれます。絵画は彼女の独特の才能です）

**3.** ＿＿＿＿＿＿ love this band for ＿＿＿＿＿＿ great songs and lively performances.
（私はこのバンドのすばらしい歌と活気のあるパフォーマンスが大好きです）

**4.** Mr. and Mrs. Smith own two houses in this district. The ones over there are ＿＿＿＿＿＿. Do you like ＿＿＿＿＿＿?
（スミス夫妻はこの地域に家を２軒所有しています。あそこにあるのが彼らの家です。あなたはそれらが気に入りましたか）

**Reading Challenger**

**A** （　　　）内のa、bから適切な語句を選び、英文を完成させましょう。その後で
音声を聞いて答えを確認しましょう。　　　　🔄 CheckLink　🎧 DL 09　◎ CD 09

Every year, my wife Sandy and ¹( **a.** I　**b.** me ) visit Japan.  Our main purpose
is shopping, and Japan is a shopper's paradise.  With its lively cities, busy markets
and trendy fashion districts, Japan offers ²( **a.** ours　**b.** us ) a unique and exciting
shopping experience.

5　　Sandy loves fashion, so Tokyo's Shibuya and Harajuku districts are ³( **a.** her
**b.** his ) favorite places to shop for clothes.  They're famous for fashionable boutiques
and trendy streetwear.  Sandy also enjoys the designer fashion and jewelry shops
in Ginza.  She likes the high fashion, but not the high prices.

A favorite area of ⁴( **a.** my　**b.** mine ) in Tokyo is Akihabara.  It's famous for
10　its electronics, gaming centers, manga, anime and unique cafés.  Akihabara has
many duty-free shops, allowing foreign visitors like ⁵( **a.** me　**b.** them ) to enjoy tax-
free shopping.

Osaka and Kyoto are also great places for shopping.  Osaka's exciting Dotonbori
area is popular for ⁶( **a.** it's　**b.** its ) huge selection of shops and delicious food.
15　Kyoto has some wonderful traditional markets, like Nishiki Market, or "Kyoto's
Kitchen."  There, we eat delicious local foods and shop for Japanese handicrafts.

**NOTES**
_____

paradise「天国」　streetwear「ストリートウェア」　electronics「電子機器」　duty-free / tax-free「免税の」
handicrafts「工芸品」

**B** 英文の内容に合うようにa〜dを並べかえ、サマリーを完成させましょう。

CheckLink

**a** Osaka's Dotonbori and Kyoto's Nishiki Market offer unique shopping experiences with delicious food and traditional handicrafts.

**b** For trendy fashion, Sandy's top shopping spots are Shibuya and Harajuku. For designer items, she goes to Ginza.

**c** The Akihabara district in Tokyo is a paradise for technology fans and lovers of video games, manga, anime and unusual cafés.

**d** Sandy and I visit Japan once a year for shopping. We enjoy its active cities and fashion districts.

**1.** ☐ ➡ **2.** ☐ ➡ **3.** ☐ ➡ **4.** ☐

**C** 英文の内容を正しく述べている文になるよう、a、bから適切な語句を選びましょう。

CheckLink

**1.** Sandy and her husband ( **a.** live   **b.** don't live ) in Japan.

**2.** Sandy's favorite shopping areas are ( **a.** Akihabara and Ginza   **b.** Harajuku and Shibuya ).

**3.** Sandy's husband likes the ( **a.** Akihabara   **b.** Asakusa ) district of Tokyo.

**4.** The Nishiki Market is in ( **a.** Kyoto   **b.** Osaka ).

# Useful Words & Phrases

**A** 右の ■ から適切な語句を選びフレーズを完成させましょう。その後で音声を聞いて答えを確認しましょう。　🎧 DL 10　◎ CD 10

1. buy a _____
2. eat local _____
3. relax on the _____
4. take a _____
5. take in the _____
6. visit a _____

> beach
> cuisine
> museum
> souvenir
> tour
> view

**B** a〜f のイラストに合うフレーズを **A** の1〜6から選び（　　）に書きましょう。

a. (　　)

b. (　　)

c. (　　)

d. (　　)

e. (　　)

f. (　　)

**C** 下の ■ から適切な語句を選び英文を完成させましょう。その後で音声を聞いて答えを確認しましょう。　🎧 DL 11　◎ CD 11

> balcony　beach　cuisine　gravy　husband　vacation　view

Every year, Jane and her ¹_____ Tim go to Hawaii for their ²_____.
They surf in the morning and relax on the ³_____ in the afternoon.  They
eat mostly local ⁴_____.  Jane likes kalua pork.  Tim enjoys loco moco.
It's rice with hamburger meat, a fried egg and ⁵_____.  After dinner, they
often sit on their hotel ⁶_____ and take in the night ⁷_____ .

**NOTE** gravy「グレービーソース」

22

# Lucky Discoveries

## 過去時制

POINT!!
● be動詞の過去形の作り方
● 一般動詞の過去形の作り方

### Reading Starter

CheckLink　DL 12　CD 12

英文を読み、話の流れに合うようにa〜dの
イラストを並べましょう。

a

One cold night in 1905, 11-year-old
Frank Epperson mistakenly left a drink
outside overnight. The next morning, he
went outside and found a frozen treat on
5 a stick. It was sweet and tasty. Frank
called his accidental creation a "popsicle"
– a combination of two words. The first
part, "pop," was from soda pop, the
drink he forgot outside the night before.
10 The second part, "sicle," came from
"icicle," describing the icy quality of the
treat. Today, millions of people around
the world enjoy Popsicles.

b

c

**NOTES**

frozen「凍った」　accidental「偶然の」
Popsicle「ポプシクル（アイスキャンディーの商標名）」
soda pop「ソーダ水」　icicle「つらら」

d

1. ☐ ➡ 2. ☐ ➡ 3. ☐ ➡ 4. ☐

# Grammar Review

## be動詞の過去形

### ▶ 形と語順

| 主語 | 肯定文 | 否定文 | 疑問文 |
|---|---|---|---|
| I / he / she / it* | I was … | I was not [I wasn't] … | Was I …? |
| you / we / they** | we were … | we were not [we weren't] … | Were we …? |

*単数名詞も同様　**複数名詞も同様

### ▶ 使い方と例文

| 名詞の前 | He was a waiter. / He wasn't a waiter. / Was he a waiter? |
|---|---|
| 形容詞の前 | The test was easy. / The test wasn't easy. / Was the test easy? |
| 前置詞＋名詞の前 | You were in class. / You weren't in class. / Were you in class? |

### ▶ 疑問文の答え方

| 肯定文 | Yes, I [he, she, it] was. / Yes, you [we, they] were. |
|---|---|
| 否定文 | No, I [he, she, it] wasn't. / No, you [we, they] weren't. |

## 一般動詞の過去形

### ▶ 形と語順

| 主語 | 肯定文 | 否定文 | 疑問文 |
|---|---|---|---|
| I / you / he / she / it / we / they* | I worked [studied, did, had, went] | I did not [didn't] work [study, do, have, go] | Did he work [study, do, have, go] …? |

*単数・複数名詞も同様

### ▶ 使い方と例文

過去形は過去に行った行動や過去に起こった出来事を言うときに使われます。一般動詞の過去形には、規則的に変化するものと不規則に変化するものがあります。規則変化する動詞は語尾に -(e)d を付けます。

**規則動詞（walk）**

Tim walked to the store. / Tim didn't walk to the store. / Did Tim walk to the store?

**不規則動詞（forget）**

Kate forgot her textbook. / Kate didn't forget her textbook. / Did Kate forget her textbook?

### ▶ 疑問文の答え方

| 肯定文 | Yes, I [you, he, she, it, we, they] did. |
|---|---|
| 否定文 | No, I [you, he, she, it, we, they] didn't. |

## 📖 Grammar Check-Up

**A** もう一度 **Reading Starter** の英文を読み、動詞の過去形に下線を引きましょう。全部で8か所見つけられますか。

**B** （　　　）内のa～cから適切な語句を選び、英文を完成させましょう。その後で音声を聞いて答えを確認しましょう。　🔗CheckLink　🎧DL 13　◎CD 13

1. Sandra and her friend ( **a.** was　**b.** did　**c.** were ) at the shopping mall all day.

2. Marge ( **a.** clean　**b.** cleaned　**c.** was cleaned ) the house yesterday.

3. ( **a.** Was　**b.** Were　**c.** Did ) you a good student in high school?

4. Harry ( **a.** didn't　**b.** wasn't　**c.** weren't ) happy with his test score.

5. We ( **a.** drive　**b.** driving　**c.** drove ) to the beach last Sunday.

6. I ( **a.** didn't　**b.** not　**c.** wasn't ) have time for breakfast this morning.

7. ( **a.** Did　**b.** Was　**c.** Were ) Andrew and Margaret late for the meeting?

8. ( **a.** Did you bring　**b.** Were you bring　**c.** Did you brought ) your lunch today?

## 📖 Reading Helper

日本語の意味に合うように、下の　　　から適切な語句を選び、正しい形に変えて英文を完成させましょう。マーカーを引いた語句は次ページの **Reading Challenger** に出てくる重要語句です。

| be | chop | drink | fry | give | go | make | study |
|---|---|---|---|---|---|---|---|

1. I ＿＿＿＿＿＿＿＿ to the drugstore.  The pharmacist ＿＿＿＿＿＿＿＿ me some medicine for my headache.
   （私はドラッグストアに行きました。薬剤師は私に頭痛のための薬を渡してくれました）

2. Darwin ＿＿＿＿＿＿＿＿ animals on the Galapagos Islands and ＿＿＿＿＿＿＿＿ an important discovery.
   （ダーウィンはガラパゴス諸島の動物を研究し、重大な発見をしました）

3. The chef ＿＿＿＿＿＿＿＿ the ingredients and then ＿＿＿＿＿＿＿＿ them in a hot pan.
   （シェフは食材を切り刻み、それからそれらを熱くなったフライパンで炒めました）

4. After our long hike, we ＿＿＿＿＿＿＿＿ iced tea.  It ＿＿＿＿＿＿＿＿ very refreshing.
   （長いハイキングの後で、私たちはアイスティーを飲みました。それはとても爽やかでした）

**Reading Challenger**

**A** （　　　　）内の a、b から適切な語句を選び、英文を完成させましょう。その後で
音声を聞いて答えを確認しましょう。　　　CheckLink　　DL 14　　CD 14

John Pemberton [1]( **a.** was  **b.** were ) a pharmacist from Atlanta, Georgia.  One day in 1886, he mixed together some ingredients for the purpose of creating a medicine for headaches.  He then tasted the blend and was happily surprised by its unique and refreshing flavor.

5　　Pemberton improved the recipe and [2]( **a.** drank  **b.** sold ) it as a syrup to local pharmacies and restaurants.  In those days, pharmacies commonly had counters for customers to enjoy sodas, ice cream, milkshakes and other treats.  The staff mixed the syrup with carbonated water and then [3]( **a.** ordered  **b.** served ) the drinks to customers.

10　　Customers loved the fizzy beverage, and sales grew quickly over the next few years.  Sadly, however, Pemberton [4]( **a.** dead  **b.** died ) in 1888 at age 57.  In 1892, his business partner made a company.  He gave the company the same name as the beverage – Coca-Cola.  Pemberton [5]( **a.** choose  **b.** chose ) the name to express the drink's key ingredients: coca leaves and kola nuts.

15　　Pemberton never [6]( **a.** achieved  **b.** didn't achieve ) his goal of creating a medicine for headaches.  But his accidental discovery greatly changed the way people enjoy drinks.

---

**NOTES**

improve「…を改良する」　syrup「シロップ」　carbonated water「炭酸水」　fizzy beverage「炭酸飲料」

B 英文の内容に合うようにa～dを並べかえ、サマリーを完成させましょう。

🔄CheckLink

**a** Pemberton made some changes to the recipe and then supplied it as a syrup to pharmacies and restaurants. They added carbonated water and served the drink to customers.

**b** In 1886, John Pemberton mixed some ingredients together with the goal of making a medicine for headaches. To his surprise, he liked the taste.

**c** Pemberton was unsuccessful at making a headache medicine, but people loved his discovery. And they still do today.

**d** After Pemberton's death, his business partner started a company and named it Coca-Cola. It was the same name Pemberton gave his drink in 1886.

1. ☐ ➡ 2. ☐ ➡ 3. ☐ ➡ 4. ☐

C 英文の内容を正しく述べている文になるよう、a、bから適切な語句を選びましょう。

🔄CheckLink

1. John Pemberton was a ( a. pharmacist   b. restaurant owner ) in Atlanta.

2. Pharmacies and restaurants ( a. bought Pemberton's recipe   b. used Pemberton's syrup ) and made drinks for customers.

3. ( a. Pemberton's business partner   b. Pemberton and his business partner ) created the Coca-Cola Company.

4. Coca-Cola's key ingredients are ( a. coca seeds and kola leaves   b. coca leaves and kola nuts ).

# Useful Words & Phrases

**A** 右の⬜️から適切な語句を選びフレーズを完成させましょう。その後で音声を
聞いて答えを確認しましょう。　🎧 DL 15　💿 CD 15

1. be a stroke of _____
2. conduct an _____
3. discover a hidden _____
4. give it a _____
5. have a chance _____
6. have a lightbulb _____

> experiment
> luck
> meeting
> moment
> talent
> try

**B** a～f のイラストに合うフレーズを **A** の1～6から選び（　　）に書きましょう。

a. (　　　)

b. (　　　)

c. (　　　)

d. (　　　)

e. (　　　)

f. (　　　)

**C** 下の⬜️から適切な語句を選び英文を完成させましょう。その後で音声を聞いて
答えを確認しましょう。　🎧 DL 16　💿 CD 16

> art　brush　luck　meeting　talent　thinking　try

One day, Sandra had a chance [1]_____ with an artist.  He talked about
his love for [2]_____, and asked Sandra to join his painting class.  Without
[3]_____, she said, "OK, I'll give it a [4]_____."  The next day, Sandra went
to the class and excitedly held a [5]_____ in her hand.  To her surprise, she soon
discovered her hidden [6]_____ as a painter.  It was a stroke of [7]_____!

28

# Unit 4

# Saving Our Precious Water

## 名詞

POINT!!

● 可算名詞と不可算名詞の違い
● 数量を表す語句の使い分け

## Reading Starter

CheckLink  DL 17  CD 17

英文を読み、話の流れに合うようにa～dの
イラストを並べましょう。

Water waste is a major problem in many
parts of the world.  For example, in the
United States, the average person uses
around 300 liters of water per day.  In
5 Japan, the number is about 250 liters,
or one bathtub full of water every day.
That's a lot!  Many people use large
amounts of water for taking showers or
baths, washing dishes, doing laundry
10 and flushing the toilet.  However, water
is precious.  It's important that we save
it for future generations and for the
health of the Earth.

**NOTES**

water waste「水の無駄遣い」
flushing the toilet「トイレの水を流すこと」
generations「世代」

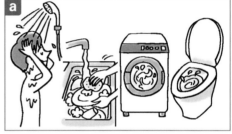

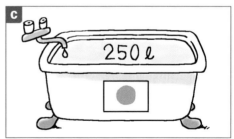

1. ☐ ➡ 2. ☐ ➡ 3. ☐ ➡ 4. ☐

29

# Grammar Review

## 可 算 名 詞

可算名詞とは、例えば「1冊の本」「2人の男の子」など数えられる名詞のことです。

単数名詞：An **orange** is on the table.　　複数名詞：**Oranges** are on the table.

### ▶ 複数形の作り方

| | |
|---|---|
| 語尾に -s をつける | pen → pen**s** / apple → apple**s** / student → student**s** |
| 語尾に -es をつける<br>（s, ss, sh, ch, o, x で終わる名詞） | peach → peach**es** / class → class**es** / dish → dish**es** /<br>watch → watch**es** / potato → potato**es** / box → box**es** |
| 語尾を変えて -(e)s をつける<br>（子音字 +y, f, fe で終わる名詞） | baby → bab**ies** / party → part**ies** / scarf → scar**ves** /<br>leaf → lea**ves** / life → li**ves** / knife → kni**ves** |
| 不規則変化する名詞 | man → **men** / woman → **women** / person → **people**<br>/ child → **children** / tooth → **teeth** / foot → **feet** |

## 不 可 算 名 詞

不可算名詞とは、例えば「牛乳」「幸せ」など数えられない名詞のことです。
不可算名詞は単数扱いです。　　○ Milk is healthy.　× Milk are healthy.

### ▶ 不可算名詞のカテゴリ

| | |
|---|---|
| 物質名詞 | water, rice, meat, plastic, wood, sand, snow, gold, soap |
| 抽象名詞 | time, information, weather, work, advice, money, music |
| 集合名詞 | food, fruit, furniture, luggage, jewelry, equipment |

### ▶ 可算名詞や不可算名詞に用いられる量詞（数量を表す語句）

| | |
|---|---|
| many / a few（少数の）/ few（ほとんどない）<br>＋複数可算名詞 | Many **people** are in the zoo today.<br>今日はたくさんの人が動物園にいます。 |
| much* / a little（少量の）/ little（ほとんどない）<br>＋不可算名詞 | There is a little **tea** in the cup.<br>カップには少し紅茶が入っています。 |
| some / any** / a lot of / lots of<br>＋複数可算名詞または不可算名詞 | He has a lot of **hats**.<br>彼はたくさんの帽子を持っています。<br>She has lots of **jewelry**.<br>彼女はたくさんの宝石を持っています。 |

*much は一般的に否定文で使われます。 There isn't **much** coffee in the pot.

** any は否定文と疑問文で使います。 We don't have **any** eggs. / Do we have **any** fruit?

## Grammar Check-Up

**A** もう一度**Reading Starter**の英文を読み、複数可算名詞に下線を引きましょう。全部で9か所見つけられますか。

**B** （　　　）内のa～cから適切な語句を選び、英文を完成させましょう。その後で音声を聞いて答えを確認しましょう。　⟳**CheckLink** 🎧 DL 18 ◎ CD 18

1. Debbie has three ( **a.** sister   **b.** sisters   **c.** a sister ).

2. Bobby likes ( **a.** meat   **b.** a meat   **c.** meats ) very much.

3. I usually eat ( **a.** sandwich   **b.** a sandwich   **c.** some sandwich ) for lunch.

4. Do you play ( **a.** a   **b.** much   **c.** any ) sports?

5. Zack listens to ( **a.** music   **b.** a music   **c.** many music ) on the bus.

6. There is ( **a.** some   **b.** any   **c.** a few ) fruit on the table.

7. Janet studies ( **a.** a few   **b.** a little   **c.** much ) hours every night.

8. There isn't ( **a.** an   **b.** any   **c.** many ) information about the accident.

## Reading Helper

日本語の意味に合うように、下の▢▢から適切な語句を選び、必要に応じて形を変えて英文を完成させましょう。マーカーを引いた語句は次ページの**Reading Challenger**に出てくる重要語句です。

| coffee | cookie | floor | game | garage | homework | money | thing |

1. I have many bad habits.  For instance, I always drink _____ and eat a
   few _____ before bed.
   (私には悪い習慣がたくさんあります。例えば、寝る前にいつもコーヒーを飲んだりクッキーを少し食べたりします)

2. Don't spend all your _____ on unnecessary _____.  Use it wisely.
   (不必要なものにお金を全部使ってはいけません。賢くそれを使いなさい)

3. Instead of doing his _____, Ron played video _____.
   (ロンは宿題をしないでテレビゲームをしました)

4. We have two brooms – one for our kitchen _____, the other for our
   _____.
   (私たちはほうきを2本持っています。1本は台所の床用で、もう1本は車庫用です)

31

A （　　）内のa、bから適切な語句を選び、英文を完成させましょう。その後で
音声を聞いて答えを確認しましょう。　　　CheckLink　　DL 19　　CD 19

Using water wisely is important for protecting this precious resource. As
individuals, we have the power to make a difference, starting by reducing our
personal water usage. Here are some ¹( **a.** idea **b.** ideas ).

First, consider your bathing habits. For example, reduce your shower time.
5 Wash your ²( **a.** hair **b.** hairs ) with the water off, and then turn it on again to
rinse. Fill your bathtub with less water. Second, wash full loads of clothes instead
of only a few items at a time. All of these ³( **a.** action **b.** actions ) save water.

In addition to the ⁴( **a.** suggestion **b.** suggestions ) above, find other ways of
doing things that usually require water. For example, instead of using water
10 to clean outdoor areas, use a ⁵( **a.** broom **b.** brooms ) to sweep your terrace or
sidewalk. After using water, find ways to repurpose it, or use it again. For
instance, reuse bathwater to water ⁶( **a.** plant **b.** plants ) or wash floors.

By changing some of our habits and using a little creativity, it's possible for all
of us to reduce our water usage and protect our resources.

**NOTES**

resource「資源」　bathing「入浴」　loads「（機械が一度に処理できる）量」　at a time「一度に」　sweep「…を掃く」
sidewalk「歩道」　repurpose「…を再利用する」

**B** 英文の内容に合うようにa〜dを並べかえ、サマリーを完成させましょう。

CheckLink

**a** Repurpose water or find other ways to do tasks that normally require water.

**b** Changing the way we bathe and wash our clothes saves water.

**c** Simple changes in our habits and a bit of creativity allow us to use less water and protect the water supply.

**d** Our water resources need protection. A good start is for individuals to use less water.

**1.** ☐ ➡ **2.** ☐ ➡ **3.** ☐ ➡ **4.** ☐

**C** 英文の内容を正しく述べている文になるよう、a、bから適切な語句を選びましょう。

CheckLink

**1.** The passage suggests ( a. reducing our shower time   b. showering instead of bathing ).

**2.** The passage suggests ( a. washing clothes once a week   b. washing only full loads of clothes ).

**3.** The passage suggests using ( a. less water   b. a broom ) to clean outdoor areas.

**4.** Repurposing water means ( a. reusing water for different uses   b. using small amounts of water ).

# Useful Words & Phrases

**A** 右の▨から適切な語句を選びフレーズを完成させましょう。その後で音声を聞いて答えを確認しましょう。　🎧 DL 20　💿 CD 20

1. fix a water _____
2. leave the water _____
3. pay the water _____
4. run a _____
5. saving water means saving _____
6. turn off the _____

> bath
> bill
> faucet
> leak
> money
> running

**B** a～f のイラストに合うフレーズを **A** の1～6から選び（　）に書きましょう。

a. (　　)

b. (　　)

c. (　　)

d. (　　)

e. (　　)

f. (　　)

**C** 下の▨から適切な語句を選び、必要に応じて形を変えて英文を完成させましょう。その後で音声を聞いて答えを確認しましょう。　🎧 DL 21　💿 CD 21

> bathtub　faucet　liter　money　running　time　tooth

It's surprising, but many people brush their [1]_____ and don't turn off the [2]_____. Every [3]_____ a person brushes and leaves the water [4]_____, they waste water. In one year, that adds up to three or four thousand [5]_____. That's enough water to fill 15 or 20 [6]_____! And remember, water isn't free. Saving water means saving [7]_____.

34

# Unit 5

# Festival Fun and Games

## 前置詞

 POINT!!
● 前置詞の役割
● 前置詞の種類とそれぞれの意味

## Reading Starter

CheckLink  DL 22  CD 22

英文を読み、話の流れに合うようにa～dの
イラストを並べましょう。

La Tomatina is a famous summer
festival in Buñol, Spain, a small town
near Valencia.  It takes place on the
last Wednesday in August every year.

5 The festival begins with the *Palo
Jabón* climbing contest.  "Palo Jabón"
means "greased pole" in Spanish.  Most
climbers slip and fall.  The first person
to successfully climb the slippery

10 pole and take the ham at the top is
the winner.  After that, trucks full of
tomatoes arrive at the festival area.
Then the real fun begins – a huge, wild,
exciting, joyful and very messy tomato

15 food fight!

**NOTES**

take place「行われる」 greased pole「油を塗った柱」
slip「滑る」 slippery「滑りやすい」 messy「乱雑な」
food fight「フードファイト（食べ物を投げ合う催し）」

**1.** ☐ ➡ **2.** ☐ ➡ **3.** ☐ ➡ **4.** ☐

35

# Grammar Review

前置詞は、名詞や代名詞と一緒に使われて前置詞句を形成し、物の位置や場所、時を表すために用いられます。前置詞は常に名詞や代名詞の前に置かれます。

| 場所を表す前置詞 | in the park / on the table | 時を表す前置詞 | at 1:00 / in May |

## 場所を表す前置詞

| | |
|---|---|
| **at**「…に、…で」<br>She works **at** the hospital. | **under**「…の下に」<br>There's a bench **under** the tree. |
| **to**「…へ」<br>Jeff takes a bus **to** school. | **over**「…の上に」<br>The bridge goes **over** the river. |
| **in**「…（の中）に」<br>Helen is **in** the garden. | **in front of**「…の前に」<br>A coffee table is **in front of** the sofa. |
| **on**「…（の上）に」<br>Butter is **on** the counter. | **behind**「…の後ろに」<br>A big dog is **behind** you. |
| **near**「…の近くに」<br>The hotel is **near** the airport. | **between**「…の間に」<br>Nagoya is **between** Tokyo and Osaka. |
| **along**「…に沿って」<br>Many people walk **along** the lake. | **through**「…を通って」<br>Let's walk home **through** the park. |
| **beside / next to**「…のとなりに、…のそばに」<br>The plant is **beside** the window.<br>My alarm clock is **next to** my bed. | **across from / opposite**「…の向かいに」<br>The bank is **across from** the library.<br>The café is **opposite** the bookstore. |

## 時を表す前置詞

| | |
|---|---|
| **at**「…に（時刻・ある時間）」<br>See you **at** 12:00 [**at** lunchtime]. | **before**「…の前に」<br>Ben goes jogging **before** breakfast. |
| **in**「…に（年・月・季節・午前・午後）」<br>Classes start **in** April [**in** spring]. | **during**「…の間中（ずっと）」<br>Sam fell asleep **during** the movie. |
| **on**「…に（曜日・日付）」<br>The game is **on** Sunday [**on** July 1]. | **after**「…の後に」<br>Everyone was tired **after** the meeting. |
| **for**「…の間（期間）」<br>Let's take a break **for** 10 minutes. | **until**「…まで（ずっと）」<br>Mari did homework **until** 2 a.m. |
| **from ... to ~**「…から~まで」<br>Carla works **from** 8 a.m. **to** 5 p.m. | **by**「…までに」<br>The boss needs my report **by** Friday. |

## Grammar Check-Up

**A**  もう一度 **Reading Starter** の英文を読み、場所を表す前置詞には下線を、時を表す前置詞には波線を引きましょう。全部で7か所見つけられますか。

**B**  (    ) 内の a ～ c から適切な語句を選び、英文を完成させましょう。その後で音声を聞いて答えを確認しましょう。　⟳ CheckLink　🎧 DL 23　◉ CD 23

1.  Please return ( **a.** in　**b.** to　**c.** on ) your seats.

2.  Let's meet ( **a.** at　**b.** between　**c.** to ) the restaurant.

3.  Don't walk ( **a.** over　**b.** on　**c.** through ) the forest at night.

4.  Brad and Yvonne got married ( **a.** at　**b.** in　**c.** on ) February 12.

5.  Some of the boys play soccer ( **a.** by　**b.** during　**c.** to ) their lunch break.

6.  Please come home ( **a.** by　**b.** for　**c.** until ) 10 o'clock.

7.  There's a nice museum ( **a.** across　**b.** in front　**c.** next ) from the station.

8.  Anne exercises ( **a.** during　**b.** at　**c.** for ) two hours every day.


## Reading Helper

日本語の意味に合うように、下の▭から適切な語句を選び英文を完成させましょう。
マーカーを引いた語句は次ページの **Reading Challenger** に出てくる重要語句です。

| after | during | for | in | in front of | near | on | under |
|-------|--------|-----|-----|-------------|------|-----|-------|

1.  The police found some weapons _____ a bridge _____ the town.
    (警察はその町の近くにある橋の下で凶器をいくつか見つけました)

2.  _____ dinner, I watched an interesting TV program about famous people _____ the 20th century.
    (夕食の後で私は20世紀の有名な人々についての興味深いテレビ番組を見ました)

3.  Please write down your concerns _____ the paper _____ you.
    (あなたの前にある紙に懸案事項を書き留めてください)

4.  _____ the meeting, the restaurant manager talked about food waste _____ 30 minutes.
    (会議の間、レストランの経営者は30分間食品廃棄物について話しました)

**Reading Challenger**

**A** （　　　）内のa、bから適切な語句を選び、英文を完成させましょう。その後で
音声を聞いて答えを確認しましょう。　 CheckLink　DL 24　CD 24

Every summer, thousands of people from all over the world travel [1]( **a.** at　**b.** to )
Buñol, Spain for the La Tomatina festival and its world-famous tomato food fight.
The festival began around the middle of the 20th century.　One popular story
suggests that a playful food fight started [2]( **a.** during　**b.** until ) a parade [3]( **a.** by
5　**b.** in ) the 1940s, and people used tomatoes as their "weapons."

Usually 20,000 to 40,000 people participate in the La Tomatina tomato food
fight.　The fight starts [4]( **a.** at　**b.** in ) 11 a.m., and lasts [5]( **a.** during　**b.** for ) about
one hour.　But the festival isn't just a food fight.　A parade, music, dancing and
other fun activities also take place throughout the day.

10　Some people have concerns about food waste and the cleanliness of the
festival.　However, the festival uses only inedible tomatoes – they're all very soft
or damaged.　As for cleanliness, volunteers and city workers carefully clean the
streets [6]( **a.** before　**b.** after ) the event.

Participants of the festival describe La Tomatina as a unique and thrilling
15　experience.　It makes many of them feel young again and creates lifelong
memories.

**NOTES**

participate in ...「…に参加する」　throughout「…の間中」　cleanliness「清潔さ」　inedible「食べられない」
damaged「傷んだ」　participants「参加者」　thrilling「スリル満点の」

38

**B** 英文の内容に合うようにa〜dを並べかえ、サマリーを完成させましょう。

CheckLink

**a** La Tomatina is a unique and exciting experience for participants. They leave the festival with wonderful memories.

**b** Many people visit Buñol, Spain every year for La Tomatina, a festival that began in the mid-20th century.

**c** Some people worry about food waste and cleanliness, but La Tomatina uses inedible tomatoes, and people clean the streets after the food fight.

**d** In addition to the popular La Tomatina food fight, the festival offers a variety of other enjoyable events.

**1.** ☐ ➡ **2.** ☐ ➡ **3.** ☐ ➡ **4.** ☐

**C** 英文の内容を正しく述べている文になるよう、a、bから適切な語句を選びましょう。

CheckLink

**1.** La Tomatina is a ( **a.** spring   **b.** summer ) festival.

**2.** One story suggests that a food fight began ( **a.** at a food festival   **b.** during a parade ) in Buñol in the 1940s.

**3.** The La Tomatina tomato food fight continues for ( **a.** one hour   **b.** one day ).

**4.** The festival's tomatoes are ( **a.** safe   **b.** unsafe ) to eat.

# Useful Words & Phrases

**A** 右の▯から適切な語句を選びフレーズを完成させましょう。その後で音声を聞いて答えを確認しましょう。　🎧 DL 25　💿 CD 25

1. _____ a folding fan
2. _____ octopus dumplings
3. _____ goldfish scooping
4. _____ in a light cotton kimono and wooden sandals
5. _____ to traditional festival music
6. _____ with shaved ice

> cool off
> dance
> dress up
> eat
> play
> use

**B** a〜f のイラストに合うフレーズを **A** の1〜6から選び（　　）に書きましょう。

a. (　　)　　b. (　　)　　c. (　　)

d. (　　)　　e. (　　)　　f. (　　)

**C** 下の▯から適切な語句を選び英文を完成させましょう。その後で音声を聞いて答えを確認しましょう。　🎧 DL 26　💿 CD 26

> cool off　　dance　　dress up　　eat　　look forward to　　play　　take place

During the summer months, people in Japan ¹_____ lively summer festivals. These joyful events ²_____ in parks, temples and streets across the country. People ³_____ to traditional festival music, ⁴_____ delicious hot food, ⁵_____ with shaved ice and ⁶_____ goldfish scooping and other fun games. They often ⁷_____ in light cotton kimonos and wooden sandals.

# Work Pre- and Post-COVID-19

進行形

POINT!!
- 現在進行形と過去進行形の作り方
- 進行形の否定文と疑問文の形

 **Reading Starter**

CheckLink  DL 27  CD 27

英文を読み、話の流れに合うようにa〜dの
イラストを並べましょう。

Before COVID-19, businesses in Japan
were operating as usual. Salaried
workers were getting up early, riding
crowded trains and arriving at their
5 workplace with sleepy eyes. During
the day, they were typing on keyboards,
discussing projects and attending
meetings. Overtime was common, and
many people were working late into the
10 evening. Others were enjoying meals
or drinks with co-workers after regular
business hours. But all that changed
with COVID-19. Suddenly, trains
weren't carrying many people, offices and
15 restaurants were quiet and nearly empty,
and remote work was becoming the new
working standard.

**NOTES**

operating「営業している」 as usual「平常どおり」
salaried workers「サラリーマン」 overtime「時間外
労働、残業」 co-workers「同僚」 empty「空いている、
人のいない」 remote work「リモートワーク」

1. ☐ ➡ 2. ☐ ➡ 3. ☐ ➡ 4. ☐

# Grammar Review

## 現在進行形

現在進行形は以下のようなときに使用されます。

**❶ 話者が話しているのと同時に行われている動作・行為を述べるとき**

Jim is talking to Linda. (ジムはリンダと話しています)

**❷ 比較的長い期間において進行中で完了していない動作・行為を述べるとき**

They are planning a trip to Canada. (彼らは (最近) カナダへの旅行を計画しています)

▶ **形と語順：**〈be動詞の現在形＋動詞のing形〉

| 主語 | 肯定文 | 否定文 | 疑問文 |
|---|---|---|---|
| I | I'm reading … | I'm not reading … | Am I reading …? |
| you / we / they | we're reading … | we aren't reading … | Are we reading …? |
| he / she / it | he's reading … | he isn't reading … | Is he reading …? |

※ know, have, love などの動詞は、動作動詞ではないため、現在進行形では使用されません。

×I'm having a car. ○I have a car. / ×He is loving her. ○He loves her.

▶ **例文**

| 現在行われていること | Jo's making lunch. / Jo isn't making lunch. / Is Jo making lunch?<br>I'm talking to Sue. / I'm not talking to Sue. / Am I talking to Sue? |
|---|---|
| 最近行われていること | Al's writing a book. / Al isn't writing a book. / Is Al writing a book?<br>We're learning art. / We aren't learning art. / Are we learning art? |

※ now「今」、right now「今のところ」、at the moment「現在」は、現在進行形と一緒によく使われます。

She's looking at a map now [right now, at the moment].

## 過去進行形

過去進行形は、過去において進行中の動作・行為を述べるときに使用されます。

I was watching television. (私はテレビを見ていました)

▶ **形と語順：**〈be動詞の過去形＋動詞のing形〉

| 主語 | 肯定文 | 否定文 | 疑問文 |
|---|---|---|---|
| I / he / she / it | she was sleeping | she wasn't sleeping | Was she sleeping? |
| you / we / they | we were sleeping | we weren't sleeping | Were we sleeping? |

▶ **例文**

He was playing a game. / He wasn't playing a game. / Was he playing a game?
You were living in Kobe. / You weren't living in Kobe. / Were you living in Kobe?

※ then「その時」、at that time「その当時 [時刻]」は、過去進行形と一緒によく使われます。

I was walking home then [at that time, at 6 o'clock].

## Grammar Check-Up

**A** もう一度 **Reading Starter** の英文を読み、進行形〈be動詞＋動詞のing形〉に下線を引きましょう。全部で11か所見つけられますか。be動詞が省略されている場合もあります。

**B** (　　　　) 内の a ～ c から適切な語句を選び、英文を完成させましょう。その後で音声を聞いて答えを確認しましょう。　　　　 ↻ CheckLink 🎧 DL 28 ◎ CD 28

1. I ( **a.** waiting　　**b.** am waiting　　**c.** are waiting ) for a taxi.

2. ( **a.** Is it raining　　**b.** Is it's raining　　**c.** Is raining it ) now?

3. Kara ( **a.** were　　**b.** isn't　　**c.** was ) working at a bank at that time.

4. These days, ( **a.** I'm not　　**b.** I don't　　**c.** I wasn't ) eating very much.

5. ( **a.** Was　　**b.** Are　　**c.** Were ) Jack and his son hiking in the mountains then?

6. We ( **a.** eating dinner　　**b.** were dinner eating　　**c.** were eating dinner ) then.

7. My TV was on, but ( **a.** I was　　**b.** I'm not　　**c.** I wasn't) watching it.

8. Is ( **a.** taking a test Jane　　**b.** Jane taking a test　　**c.** a test taking Jane )?

## Reading Helper

日本語の意味に合うように、下の ▭ から適切な語句を選び、現在進行形・過去進行形に変えて英文を完成させましょう（否定文の場合もあります）。マーカーを引いた語句は次ページの **Reading Challenger** に出てくる重要語句です。

| drive | get | sleep | work |

1. Jake ＿＿＿＿＿＿＿＿ to the beach yesterday and he had an accident. Fortunately, no one was hurt.
（ジェイクは昨日ビーチまでドライブをしていて事故を起こしました。幸運にも誰もけがをしませんでした）

2. Oh, no!  My computer ＿＿＿＿＿＿＿ again.  It isn't very reliable.
（何てこと！　私のパソコンがまた動かないです。それはあまり頼りになりません）

3. These days, I ＿＿＿＿＿＿＿ much satisfaction from my club activity.
（最近私は部活動にあまり満足を得ていません）

4. The meeting wasn't very productive.  Some members at the back of the room
＿＿＿＿＿＿＿ .
（会議はあまり生産的ではありませんでした。部屋の後ろにいた何人かのメンバーが寝ていました）

**Reading Challenger**

A ( ) 内の a、b から適切な語句を選び、英文を完成させましょう。その後で
音声を聞いて答えを確認しましょう。 🔄 CheckLink 🎧 DL 29 💿 CD 29

Fortunately, COVID-19 isn't a major concern in Japan anymore, and workers
are making their daily commutes to the office again. However, many people are
still ¹( **a.** doing **b.** working ) from their homes, or ²( **a.** dividing **b.** using ) their
work time between their homes and offices.

5 Companies are adjusting to the new working style and ³( **a.** controlling
**b.** supporting ) remote workers. For example, many companies are providing
workers with reliable internet connections, laptop computers and the necessary
software to do their work online.

In addition, an increasing number of companies are offering flexible work
10 hours. This enables workers to have some control over their schedules, manage
their work effectively and enjoy a healthy work-life balance. This flexibility is
⁴( **a.** boosting **b.** decreasing ) many workers' job satisfaction and improving their
work performance.

Remote work has its challenges, too. Some workers are ⁵( **a.** having **b.** making )
15 trouble separating their work time and relaxation time. Others are missing the face-
to-face communication they enjoyed in the office. In addition, some workers ⁶( **a.** are
being **b.** are not being ) very productive, as household work and small children make
it difficult for them to focus on their work.

---

**NOTES**

daily commutes「毎日の通勤」 adjusting to ...「…に順応している」 flexible「柔軟な」 effectively「効果的に」

44

**B** 英文の内容に合うようにa〜dを並べかえ、サマリーを完成させましょう。

CheckLink

**a** Companies are adjusting to remote work by providing workers with equipment and support such as internet connections and laptops for online work.

**b** Challenges of remote work for some workers include difficulty in maintaining a work-life balance, limited face-to-face conversations and reduced productivity.

**c** After COVID-19, workers are once again commuting to work every day.  Others continue with remote work, or divide their time between their homes and offices.

**d** More companies are giving workers flexible work hours, leading to increased job satisfaction and improved performance.

**1.** ☐ ➡ **2.** ☐ ➡ **3.** ☐ ➡ **4.** ☐

**C** 英文の内容を正しく述べている文になるよう、a、bから適切な語句を選びましょう。

CheckLink

**1.** Some companies are sending ( **a.** desktop     **b.** laptop ) computers to workers' homes.

**2.** Flexible work hours ( **a.** give workers more time to finish projects     **b.** allow workers to set their own schedules ).

**3.** Remote work does not allow for ( **a.** face-to-face communication     **b.** relaxation time ).

**4.** According to the passage, a challenge for some remote workers is ( **a.** balancing their work and leisure time    **b.** working alone ).

# Useful Words & Phrases

**A** 右の ■ から適切な語句を選びフレーズを完成させましょう。その後で音声を聞いて答えを確認しましょう。

🎧 DL 30　💿 CD 30

1. be _____

2. do _____

3. meet a _____

4. punch a _____

5. put in _____

6. work at your own _____

deadline
overtime
pace
paperwork
self-employed
time card

**B** a〜f のイラストに合うフレーズを **A** の1〜6から選び（　　）に書きましょう。

a. (　　)　　　　　b. (　　)　　　　　c. (　　)

d. (　　)　　　　　e. (　　)　　　　　f. (　　)

**C** 下の ■ から適切な語句を選び英文を完成させましょう。その後で音声を聞いて答えを確認しましょう。

🎧 DL 31　💿 CD 31

commutes　family　flexibility　overtime　pace　paperwork　self-employed

In my old job, I was putting in [1] _____ every day and doing [2] _____ nonstop. It was very tiring and stressful. But now, things are different. I'm [3] _____ and working from home. No more long [4] _____ for me! I'm working at my own [5] _____. My new job gives me freedom and [6] _____, and more time with my [7] _____. I love it!

46

# Online Social Gaming

**Unit 7**

不定詞と動名詞

POINT!!
● 不定詞と動名詞の形
● 動詞の目的語としての不定詞と動名詞

## Reading Starter

 CheckLink  DL 32  CD 32

英文を読み、話の流れに合うようにa～dの
イラストを並べましょう。

Millions of people worldwide enjoy playing online games with members of the same online group, in other words, social gaming. At first, most
5 people prefer doing it with friends or family members. Then, after gaining confidence, they often decide to participate with strangers from different parts of the world. Japan has an exciting
10 and active social gaming scene, with a strong focus on smartphone and tablet devices. The market for social games in Japan continues to grow, with new games and features, and regular updates and
15 events.

**NOTES**

social gaming「ソーシャルゲームをすること」
confidence「自信」 strangers「知らない人」
devices「デバイス、装置」 features「目玉商品」
updates「アップデート、更新」

1. ☐ ➡ 2. ☐ ➡ 3. ☐ ➡ 4. ☐

47

# Grammar Review

不定詞と動名詞は「…すること」という意味を表し、動詞の目的語としてよく使われます。動詞の中には不定詞または動名詞の一方のみを目的語にとるものもあれば、不定詞と動名詞の両方を目的語にとるものもあります。

---

不定詞の作り方 ➡ 〈to＋動詞の原形〉

Mary likes **to draw** pictures.（メアリーは絵を描くことが好きです）

---

## 不定詞のみを目的語にとる動詞

**choose decide hope learn need plan promise want** など

Emily **decided to study** in England.（エミリーはイングランドで勉強することを決めました）

He **needs to return** his library book.（彼は図書館の本を返す必要があります）

I **promise to call** you later.（後であなたに電話することを約束します）

---

動名詞の作り方 ➡ 〈動詞の原形＋-ing〉

Bruce enjoys **playing** sports.（ブルースはスポーツをすることを楽しんでいます）

---

## 動名詞のみを目的語にとる動詞

**dislike enjoy finish keep mind practice quit suggest** など

Michelle **dislikes getting up** early.（ミシェルは早起きすることが嫌いです）

I **don't mind working** on weekends.（私は週末に仕事をすることが気になりません）

Alan **quit smoking** last year.（アランは去年禁煙しました）

---

## 不定詞と動名詞の両方を目的語にとる動詞

**begin continue hate like love prefer start** など

It **began to snow** [**snowing**] a few minutes ago.（数分前に雪が降り始めました）

Let's **continue to study** [**studying**] after dinner.（夕食後に勉強を続けましょう）

Shelly **loves to sing** [**singing**].（シェリーは歌うことが大好きです）

---

## Grammar Check-Up

**A** もう一度**Reading Starter**の英文を読み、〈動詞＋不定詞〉と〈動詞＋動名詞〉に下線を引きましょう。全部で４か所見つけられますか。

**B** （　　　）内のa〜cから適切な語句を選び、英文を完成させましょう。その後で音声を聞いて答えを確認しましょう。　**CheckLink**　**DL 33**　**CD 33**

1. Jennifer hopes ( **a.** to travel　**b.** traveling　**c.** aまたはb ) to Italy someday.
2. Donald hates ( **a.** to be　**b.** being　**c.** aまたはb ) late for appointments.
3. Did you finish ( **a.** to write　**b.** writing　**c.** aまたはb ) your blog?
4. We plan ( **a.** to have　**b.** having　**c.** aまたはb ) dinner after the movie.
5. Fiona practices ( **a.** to play　**b.** playing　**c.** aまたはb ) the piano every day.
6. I learned ( **a.** to surf　**b.** surfing　**c.** aまたはb ) during my vacation in Hawaii.
7. Do you prefer ( **a.** to work　**b.** working　**c.** aまたはb ) alone or in a group?
8. Our teacher suggested ( **a.** to study　**b.** studying　**c.** aまたはb ) the vocabulary list before the test.

## Reading Helper

日本語の意味に合うように、下の　　　から適切な語句を選び、必要に応じて形を変えて英文を完成させましょう。マーカーを引いた語句は次ページの**Reading Challenger**に出てくる重要語句です。

| begin | decide | enjoy | plan | promise | quit | suggest | want |

1. My webcam ＿＿＿＿ working yesterday.  I ＿＿＿＿ to buy a new one today.
   （昨日私のウェブカメラが動かなくなりました。今日私は新しいものを買うつもりです）

2. The university clubs ＿＿＿＿ to do a collaboration.  They ＿＿＿＿ to discuss it next week.
   （その大学のクラブは協同することに決めました。それらはそれについて話し合うことを約束しました）

3. Ai ＿＿＿＿ doing English crossword puzzles last month.  She ＿＿＿＿ to improve her vocabulary.
   （先月アイは英語のクロスワードパズルをし始めました。彼女は語彙を増やしたいと思っています）

4. I ＿＿＿＿ traveling and adventures. – Then I ＿＿＿＿ going on an African safari.
   （私は旅行と冒険を楽しんでいます。―それなら私はアフリカのサファリに行くことを提案します）

**A** ( ) 内のa、bから適切な語句を選び、英文を完成させましょう。その後で
音声を聞いて答えを確認しましょう。　　　　　CheckLink　　DL 34　　CD 34

Young people love ¹( **a.** to go　**b.** to play ) online social games, including role-
playing games (RPGs), strategy games, puzzles, adventures and more.　For
players, the games are fun, challenging and entertaining.　In many cases, players
²( **a.** keep　**b.** mind ) playing them for hours at a time.

5　　　Social gaming connects people with similar interests.　Many participants hope
³( **a.** to form　**b.** to join ) connections with fellow gamers from different cities or
countries.　The games provide them with opportunities for collaboration, teamwork
and cooperation.　These experiences help players feel like they are part of a
friendly community.

10　　　Some social game players ⁴( **a.** like　**b.** dislike ) participating in voice chats or
video calls with other players.　For voice chats, players ⁵( **a.** need　**b.** don't need ) to
have a microphone and a speaker or headphones.　For video calls, they also need
a webcam.　Through these interactions, players share their experiences and build
friendships with other gamers.

15　　　Finally, regular updates and events in social gaming keep the games fresh
and exciting for players.　They also motivate gamers to continue ⁶( **a.** attaching
**b.** playing ) and connecting with others, and they are generally free of charge.

**NOTES**

strategy「戦略」　fellow gamers「仲間のゲーマー」　cooperation「協力」　interactions「交流、やりとり」
free of charge「無料で」

**B** 英文の内容に合うようにa〜dを並べかえ、サマリーを完成させましょう。

CheckLink

**a** Some game players enjoy voice chats and video calls with other gamers to interact, share experiences and form friendships.

**b** Updates and events keep the games interesting and fun. They also motivate players to continue playing and connecting with others.

**c** Young people enjoy playing various types of online social games. Some play for many hours without stopping.

**d** Many gamers like to connect with players from around the world, and work together with them towards a common goal.

1. ☐ ➡ 2. ☐ ➡ 3. ☐ ➡ 4. ☐

**C** 英文の内容を正しく述べている文になるよう、a、bから適切な語句を選びましょう。

CheckLink

1. RPGs means ( **a.** role-performing games   **b.** role-playing games ).

2. Online social games bring together people with ( **a.** different   **b.** the same ) interests.

3. It's ( **a.** necessary   **b.** not necessary ) for online social game players to have voice chats or video calls with other players.

4. Most updates and events in social gaming ( **a.** are free   **b.** require payment ).

# Useful Words & Phrases

**A** 右の⬛️から適切な語句を選びフレーズを完成させましょう。その後で音声を聞いて答えを確認しましょう。

🎧 DL 35　◎ CD 35

1. _____ a new character
2. _____ in-game items
3. _____ in a tournament
4. _____ a rare treasure chest
5. _____ with friends
6. _____ your character with new powers

> create
> discover
> level-up
> participate
> team up
> trade

**B** a〜f のイラストに合うフレーズを **A** の1〜6から選び（　　）に書きましょう。

a. (　　)　　　　b. (　　)　　　　c. (　　)

d. (　　)　　　　e. (　　)　　　　f. (　　)

**C** 下の⬛️から適切な語句を選び英文を完成させましょう。その後で音声を聞いて答えを確認しましょう。

🎧 DL 36　◎ CD 36

> creating　enjoy　level-up　participate　see　teaming up　work

I really $^1$_____ playing online social games and $^2$_____ characters.  It's exciting to $^3$_____ my characters with new powers and $^4$_____ them grow strong.  Playing alone is fun, but I prefer $^5$_____ with friends.  We learn to $^6$_____ together and we have a great time.  I also love to $^7$_____ in tournaments and play against other game lovers.  It's thrilling!

# Women's Social Advancement

## 現在完了形

POINT!!

● 現在完了形が表す3つの意味

● 現在完了形の作り方

## Reading Starter

CheckLink  DL 37  CD 37

英文を読み、話の流れに合うようにa～dのイラストを並べましょう。

Women's advancement in society has led to the development and progress of the United States. Over the years, women have made great gains in various
5 areas. In the late 1800s and early 1900s, women began asking for voting rights, access to education and equal opportunities. The women's liberation movement in the 1960s and 70s was
10 another strong push for women's rights and equality. During that time, women did everything from holding large parades to leading work strikes. Since then, women's status and their role in
15 society have improved greatly.

( NOTES )

advancement「進出」 voting rights「選挙権」
equal opportunities「機会の均等」
women's liberation movement「女性解放運動」
equality「平等」 strikes「ストライキ」

1. [ ] ➡ 2. [ ] ➡ 3. [ ] ➡ 4. [ ]

# Grammar Review

現在完了形は以下の目的で使われます。

❶ 過去に開始され現在もなお継続されていることを表す。

She **has worked** here for 20 years. （彼女はここで20年働いています）

I **have been** sleepy all day. （私は一日中眠いです）

❷ 現在までの経験を表す。

I **have seen** this movie before. （私はこの映画を以前見たことがあります）

Amanda **has visited** Japan 10 times. （アマンダは日本を10回訪れたことがあります）

❸ 動作が完了した結果としての現在の状態を表す。

I **have finished** my homework. （私は宿題を終えました）

The train **has** just **arrived** at the station. （その電車はちょうど駅に到着したところです）

▶ 形と語順

肯定文

| I [you, we, they] ＋ **have** [**'ve**] ＋過去分詞 ／ he [she, it] ＋ **has** [**'s**] ＋過去分詞 |
| --- |

**I've closed** the door. / **They've done** their work. / Amy **has been** to Egypt.

否定文

| I [you, we, they] ＋ **have not** [**haven't**] ＋過去分詞 ／<br>he [she, it] ＋ **has not** [**hasn't**] ＋過去分詞 |
| --- |

I **haven't closed** the door. / They **haven't done** their work. / Amy **hasn't been** to Egypt.

疑問文

| **Have** ＋ I [you, we, they] ＋過去分詞 …? ／ **Has** ＋ he [she, it] ＋過去分詞 …? |
| --- |

**Have** I **closed** the door**?** / **Have** they **done** their work**?** / **Has** Amy **been** to Egypt**?**

---

現在完了形でよく使われる語

| | |
| --- | --- |
| **for**<br>「…の間」 | 継続期間を表す<br>He **has lived** in Japan **for** 5 years. |
| **since**<br>「…以来」 | ある時点からの継続期間を表す<br>Paul and Donna **have been** married **since** 1987. |
| **already**<br>「すでに」 | 肯定文や疑問文で用いられ、現時点より前で動作が完了したことを表す<br>I've **already had** dinner. / **Have** you **already finished** your work? |
| **yet**<br>「まだ、もう」 | 否定文や疑問文で用いられ、動作がまだ完了していないことや動作の完了を<br>予期していることを表す<br>The package **hasn't arrived yet**. / **Have** you **read** the book **yet**? |
| **ever**<br>「これまでに」 | 疑問文で用いられ、経験を表す<br>**Has** he **(ever) been** to Rome? / ✕ He has ever been to Rome. |

## Grammar Check-Up

**A** もう一度 **Reading Starter** の英文を読み、現在完了形に下線を引きましょう。全部で3か所見つけられますか。

**B** （　　　）内の a ～ c から適切な語句を選び、英文を完成させましょう。その後で音声を聞いて答えを確認しましょう。　🔄CheckLink　🎧DL 38　◎CD 38

1. Cindy has ( **a.** go　**b.** gone　**c.** went ) shopping.
2. Have you ( **a.** checked　**b.** checking　**c.** been checked ) your email today?
3. ( **a.** I'm not　**b.** I'm not have　**c.** I haven't ) been to Europe.
4. ( **a.** Has found Mana　**b.** Is Mana finding　**c.** Has Mana found ) her textbook?
5. Roy has ( **a.** climbed Mt. Fuji　**b.** climbing Mt. Fuji　**c.** Mt. Fuji climbed ) twice.
6. The roses have ( **a.** already bloomed　**b.** bloomed yet　**c.** bloomed yesterday ).
7. Have ( **a.** you ever rode　**b.** ridden you ever　**c.** you ever ridden ) a horse?
8. Pat ( **a.** yet hasn't sold his house　**b.** hasn't sold his house yet　**c.** hasn't sold yet his house ).

## Reading Helper

日本語の意味に合うように、下の▢▢▢から適切な語句を選び、現在完了形に変えて英文を完成させましょう（疑問文の場合もあります）。マーカーを引いた語句は次ページの **Reading Challenger** に出てくる重要語句です。

| be | become | change | give | increase | open | read | stay |
|----|--------|--------|------|----------|------|------|------|

1. Our business strategy ＿＿＿＿ very effective. Sales ＿＿＿＿ by 20%.
   （（これまで）当社のビジネス戦略はとても効果的です。売り上げは20%伸びています）

2. A new café ＿＿＿＿ on Broad Street. – I know. Carol promoted it in her blog. ＿＿＿＿ you ＿＿＿＿ it?
   （新しいカフェがブロード・ストリートにオープンしました。—知っています。キャロルがブログで宣伝していました。あなたはそれを読んだことがありますか）

3. My boss ＿＿＿＿ me extra responsibilities, but my salary ＿＿＿＿ the same.
   （上司は私に追加の責務を与えましたが、私の給料は同じままです）

4. Do you think people's attitudes about technology ＿＿＿＿ over the years?
   –Yes, many people ＿＿＿＿ afraid of it.
   （人々の科学技術に対する態度が年々変化していると思いますか？—はい、多くの人がそれを恐れるようになっています）

**Reading Challenger**

**A** ( ) 内のa、bから適切な語句を選び、英文を完成させましょう。その後で音声を聞いて答えを確認しましょう。 CheckLink 🎧 DL 39 ◎ CD 39

The social advancement of women in Japan is still far behind other advanced countries. However, during the last 40 or 50 years, it ¹( **a.** has **b.** hasn't ) made great progress. For example, only 22% of university students were female in 1980. Today, that number has ²( **a.** reached **b.** contained ) 45%. This rise in education
5 has enabled women to choose various careers and be productive members of society.

Japanese women have also begun to hold different leadership positions. The percentage of female managers has slowly ³( **a.** fallen **b.** risen ) from 4% in 1980 to 7% today. A 2013 government policy has ⁴( **a.** been **b.** made ) effective in
10 promoting such opportunities for women.

In recent years, Japanese women have also ⁵( **a.** acted **b.** played ) active roles in politics. They have shown that they have the ability to be strong leaders. Women now make up about 10% of Diet members, up from 2.5% in 1980.

Many things have contributed to the social advancement of Japanese women.
15 They include increased access to education, changing attitudes toward gender roles and supportive policies. More childcare services, flexible work schedules and other efforts have also ⁶( **a.** allowed **b.** followed ) women to balance careers and family responsibilities.

**NOTES**

advanced countries「先進国」 female「女性（の）」 government policy「政府の方針」
politics「政治」 Diet members「国会議員」 contribute to ...「…に貢献［寄与］する」
gender roles「性差による役割」

**B** 英文の内容に合うようにa～dを並べかえ、サマリーを完成させましょう。

🔄CheckLink

**a** Japanese women's educational growth has widened their career opportunities and enabled them to actively contribute to society.

**b** Japanese women have actively participated in politics and have shown strong leadership abilities. An increasing number of women are becoming Diet members.

**c** Many important changes and supportive actions have helped Japanese women advance in society. They've also allowed them to manage both careers and families.

**d** Japanese women have made progress in holding leadership positions. A government policy has supported these opportunities.

**1.** ☐ ➡ **2.** ☐ ➡ **3.** ☐ ➡ **4.** ☐

**C** 英文の内容を正しく述べている文になるよう、a、bから適切な語句を選びましょう。

🔄CheckLink

**1.** About ( **a.** one-quarter    **b.** one-half ) of Japanese university students are female.

**2.** Seven percent of ( **a.** female Japanese workers are managers    **b.** Japanese managers are women ).

**3.** ( **a.** Ten percent of Diet members are women.    **b.** The number of female Diet members is increasing by ten percent every year. )

**4.** Views on gender roles ( **a.** are changing    **b.** haven't changed much over the years ) in Japan.

# Useful Words & Phrases

**A** 右の▨から適切な語句を選びフレーズを完成させましょう。その後で音声を聞いて答えを確認しましょう。　🎧 DL 40　💿 CD 40

1. choose a career _____
2. receive childcare _____
3. receive equal pay for equal _____
4. have gender _____
5. hold a management _____
6. enjoy a good work-life _____

balance
equality
path
position
support
work

**B** a〜fのイラストに合うフレーズを**A**の1〜6から選び（　）に書きましょう。

a. (　　　)　　　b. (　　　)　　　c. (　　　)

d. (　　　)　　　e. (　　　)　　　f. (　　　)

**C** 下の▨から適切な語句を選び英文を完成させましょう。その後で音声を聞いて答えを確認しましょう。　🎧 DL 41　💿 CD 41

> balance　leaders　pay　positions　progress　support　work

Women's social advancement in Australia has made great [1]_____ in recent years. Many women now receive equal [2]_____ for equal [3]_____. They have also received a lot more childcare [4]_____. This has allowed them to enjoy a good work-life [5]_____. In addition, more women have become strong [6]_____. In fact, many women now hold management [7]_____ in large companies.

# Unit 9

# Music Makers

## WH 疑問文

POINT!!
● WH 疑問文の作り方
● WH 疑問文で使う疑問詞の種類

## Reading Starter

CheckLink　DL 42　CD 42

英文を読み、話の流れに合うようにa〜dの
イラストを並べましょう。

❖ *What are the Grammy Awards?*
The Grammy Awards are a celebration
of major achievements in the music
industry.

5 ❖ *When did the Grammy Awards begin?*
They first took place in 1959 at the
Beverly Hilton Hotel in Beverly Hills.

❖ *What do winners get?*
Winners receive a Grammy – a small
10 golden trophy. The name "Grammy"
comes from the word "gramophone," or
record player.

❖ *Who are some famous Grammy winners?*
Seiji Ozawa for Best Opera Recording,
15 and Michael Jackson for Album of the
Year for *Thriller* are past winners.
Others include The Beatles, Coldplay
and Taylor Swift.

**NOTES**

Grammy Awards「グラミー賞」 achievements「功績」
music industry「音楽業界」 trophy「トロフィー」

**1.** [　] ➡ **2.** [　] ➡ **3.** [　] ➡ **4.** [　]

# Grammar Review

ただ単にYesかNoでの答えを求める疑問文とは違い、WH疑問文は疑問詞を使って具体的な情報や話題に関する詳細な答えを求める疑問文です。

> **When** is your lunch break?  —It's from 12:00 to 1:00.
>
> **Where** does this train go?  —It goes to Tokyo Station.

## be動詞のWH疑問文

| 疑問詞＋be動詞＋主語 | | | |
|---|---|---|---|
| **疑問詞** | **例文** | **疑問詞** | **例文** |
| who<br>「誰」 | Who is your teacher? | why<br>「なぜ」 | Why is Tina so happy? |
| what<br>「何」<br>「何の」 | What is in the bag?<br>What do you do?<br>What size are these shoes?<br>What color is your phone? | whose<br>「誰の」 | Whose pens are these? |
| | | how<br>「どのように」<br>「どのくらい」 | How was your trip?<br>How old are you?<br>How big is your apartment?<br>How far is the station?<br>How much was the taxi? |
| when<br>「いつ」 | When is the party? | | |
| where<br>「どこ」 | Where were the keys? | | |

## 一般動詞のWH疑問文

| 疑問詞＋do [does, did] ＋主語＋一般動詞の原形 | | | |
|---|---|---|---|
| **疑問詞** | **例文** | **疑問詞** | **例文** |
| who<br>「誰」 | Who do you eat lunch with? | why<br>「なぜ」 | Why did Dave quit his job? |
| what<br>「何」<br>「何の」 | What does Kelly do?<br>What do we need to buy?<br>What time did he get up?<br>What season do you like? | whose<br>「誰の」 | Whose painting do you like? |
| | | how<br>「どのように」<br>「どのくらい」 | How do you come to school?<br>How often does the bus come?<br>How many cats does he have?<br>How much does the hat cost?<br>How long did you wait? |
| when<br>「いつ」 | When does the store close? | | |
| where<br>「どこ」 | Where did you go on the weekend? | | |

※疑問詞のwhoやwhatが主語になる場合、現在時制では動詞は三人称単数現在形になります。

Who lives there? — Mrs. Miller lives there. / What scares you? — Snakes scare me.

 **Grammar Check-Up**

**A** もう一度 **Reading Starter** の英文を読み、疑問詞の答えになる部分に下線を引きましょう。全部で8か所見つけられますか。

**B** （　　　）内のa～cから適切な語句を選び、英文を完成させましょう。その後で音声を聞いて答えを確認しましょう。　　CheckLink　　DL 43　　CD 43

**1.** ( **a.** Who　**b.** When　**c.** Where ) is Margaret's birthday?

**2.** ( **a.** What　**b.** Where　**c.** How ) did you do during your vacation?

**3.** ( **a.** Whose　**b.** What time　**c.** Why ) were you absent yesterday?

**4.** ( **a.** How many　**b.** How often　**c.** How much ) do you eat sushi?

**5.** ( **a.** Where　**b.** How much　**c.** What ) did you buy your shirt?

**6.** ( **a.** Who　**b.** Where　**c.** Whose ) English class did you take last year?

**7.** ( **a.** How　**b.** What　**c.** Where ) kind of computer do you have?

**8.** Who ( **a.** did ate my ice cream　**b.** did my ice cream eat　**c.** ate my ice cream )?

## **Reading Helper**

日本語の意味に合うように、下の▢▢から適切な語句を選び英文を完成させましょう。マーカーを引いた語句は次ページの **Reading Challenger** に出てくる重要語句です。

| how | how many | what | what kind | when | where | who | why |
|-----|----------|------|-----------|------|-------|-----|-----|

**1.** ＿＿＿＿＿ did the band release its new album? ＿＿＿＿＿ is the title of the album?

(そのバンドはいつ新しいアルバムをリリースしましたか。そのアルバムのタイトルは何ですか)

**2.** ＿＿＿＿＿ causes does he work for? ＿＿＿＿＿ does he work with?

(彼はいくつの (支援) 運動のために働いていますか。彼は誰といっしょに働いていますか)

**3.** ＿＿＿＿＿ did she first achieve fame? ＿＿＿＿＿ did she manage the pressure?

(彼女はどこで最初に名声を得ましたか。彼女はどうやってプレッシャーをはねのけましたか)

**4.** ＿＿＿＿＿ is openness important for collaborations? ＿＿＿＿＿ of individuals work well on a team?

(なぜオープンであることが共同作業のために重要なのですか。どんな種類の人がチームでうまくいきますか)

A （　　　）内のa、bから適切な語句を選び、英文を完成させましょう。その後で音声を聞いて答えを確認しましょう。　　CheckLink　　DL 44　　CD 44

[1]( **a.** How **b.** Who ) is Taylor Swift?  Taylor Swift is a hugely popular American singer-songwriter and musician.  [2]( **a.** How **b.** What ) style of music does she perform?  She started her career as a country music artist in Nashville, Tennessee, but later changed her focus to pop music.

5 　　[3]( **a.** When **b.** Where ) did Taylor Swift become famous?  Swift's rise to fame began with her first album *Taylor Swift* in 2006.  She has since released many number one albums, won multiple Grammy Awards and sold millions of records worldwide.

　　[4]( **a.** How **b.** Why ) do fans like her so much?  Taylor Swift fans, or "Swifties,"
10 love her honesty, openness and great storytelling.  Her personal songs create a strong connection with her audience.  [5]( **a.** What **b.** Who ) are her songs about?  She covers themes such as love, personal growth and the advancement of women in society.

　　[6]( **a.** When **b.** Where ) has Taylor made an impact?  Not only has she made a
15 huge impact in the music industry, but she has also supported many important causes.  Some of these causes include education, poverty and cancer research.  She's an amazing person.

**NOTES**

multiple「多数の」　not only… but also ~「…だけでなく~も」　poverty「貧困」　cancer「がん」

**B** 英文の内容に合うようにa〜dを並べかえ、サマリーを完成させましょう。

**a** Taylor Swift connects with her fans through her honesty and heartfelt storytelling. She sings about love, personal development and the advancement of women.

**b** Taylor Swift is an American entertainer. She began as a country music artist, then later started performing popular music.

**c** Taylor Swift has had a big impact on music. She has also provided support to many areas of need in society.

**d** Taylor Swift gained fame with her first album in 2006. Since then, she has enjoyed continued success with albums, music awards and record sales.

**1.** ☐ ➡ **2.** ☐ ➡ **3.** ☐ ➡ **4.** ☐

**C** 英文の内容を正しく述べている文になるよう、a、bから適切な語句を選びましょう。

**1.** Taylor Swift is mainly a ( **a.** country    **b.** pop ) artist.

**2.** Swift has won ( **a.** a few    **b.** many ) Grammys.

**3.** "Swifties" are ( **a.** fans    **b.** songs ) of Taylor Swift.

**4.** According to the passage, Swift has ( **a.** written educational books
**b.** helped poor people ).

# Useful Words & Phrases

**A** 右の■から適切な語句を選びフレーズを完成させましょう。その後で音声を聞いて答えを確認しましょう。　🎧 DL 45　💿 CD 45

1. attend a _____
2. be a music _____
3. give a standing _____
4. have a front row _____
5. hit the high _____
6. perform live on _____

> concert
> lover
> notes
> ovation
> seat
> stage

**B** a〜f のイラストに合うフレーズを**A**の1〜6から選び（　）に書きましょう。

a. (　　)　　　　b. (　　)　　　　c. (　　)

d. (　　)　　　　e. (　　)　　　　f. (　　)

**C** 下の■から適切な語句を選び英文を完成させましょう。その後で音声を聞いて答えを確認しましょう。　🎧 DL 46　💿 CD 46

> artist　　concert　　fans　　lover　　seat　　songs　　stage

Annie is a music [1]_____. Recently, she attended a [2]_____ of Beyoncé, her favorite [3]_____. Annie had a front row [4]_____ and was excited to see her idol live on [5]_____. After performing for two hours, Beyoncé said good-bye, but her [6]_____ kept shouting for more. A few minutes later, she came out for an encore and sang two more [7]_____.

**NOTE** encore「アンコール」

# Unit 10

# Risks and Rewards of Online Tasks

比較級と最上級

POINT!!
● つづりが短い語の比較級と最上級の作り方
● つづりが長い語の比較級と最上級の作り方

## Reading Starter

CheckLink　DL 47　CD 47

英文を読み、話の流れに合うようにa～dの
イラストを並べましょう。

We live in a digital age. It offers a
simpler, faster and more convenient way
of doing things compared to traditional
methods. With just a few taps on our
5　smartphones, we can shop more easily.
Online hotel and airline reservations
help us find the cheapest prices and the
best deals. Viewing restaurant menus
and photos online simplifies planning for
10　lunch or dinner parties. Online banking
is another convenience of the digital age.
In short, the online world gives us the
highest level of accessibility in different
areas of our lives.

**NOTES**

digital age「デジタル時代」
compared to ...「…と比べると」
simplify「…を簡単にする」
accessibility「利用［アクセス］のしやすさ」

1. ☐ → 2. ☐ → 3. ☐ → 4. ☐

比較級 | 2つのものを比較して、「～よりも…」と言うときに使います。

形容詞の比較級 A butterfly is **lighter** than a bird.（蝶は鳥より軽いです）

副詞の比較級 She studies **harder** than me.（彼女は私よりも熱心に勉強しています）

最上級 | 3つ以上のものを比較して、「一番［最も］…」と言うときに使います。

形容詞の最上級 Tokyo is the **largest** city in Japan.（東京は日本で最大の都市です）

副詞の最上級 He ran the **fastest** in the race.（彼はレースで最も速く走りました）

## 比較級と最上級の作り方

●短い形容詞・副詞の場合：比較級は -er を、最上級は -est を語尾につけます。

| 原級（元の形） | 比較級 | 最上級 |
|---|---|---|
| cold | cold**er** | cold**est** |
| safe | saf**er** | saf**est** |
| big | big**ger** | big**gest** |
| healthy | health**ier** | health**iest** |

Today is **colder** than yesterday. / The salad is the **healthiest** item on the menu.

●長い形容詞・副詞の場合：比較級は more を、最上級は most を前につけます。

| 原級（元の形） | 比較級 | 最上級 |
|---|---|---|
| quietly | **more** quietly | **most** quietly |
| honest | **more** honest | **most** honest |
| crowded | **more** crowded | **most** crowded |
| expensive | **more** expensive | **most** expensive |

The train is **more crowded** than the bus. / It's the **most expensive** hotel in the city.

●その他の場合：比較級と最上級が不規則に変化します。

| 原級（元の形） | 比較級 | 最上級 |
|---|---|---|
| good / well | **better** | **best** |
| bad | **worse** | **worst** |
| far | **farther / further** | **farthest / furthest** |

My new phone is **better** than my old phone. / He traveled the **farthest** to get here.

**Grammar Check-Up**

**A** もう一度 **Reading Starter** の英文を読み、比較級には<u>下線</u>を、最上級には波線を引きましょう。全部で7か所見つけられますか。

**B** ( ) 内のa～cから適切な語句を選び、英文を完成させましょう。その後で音声を聞いて答えを確認しましょう。　ⅭCheckLink　🎧 DL 48　◎ CD 48

1. Milk chocolate is ( **a.** sweet　**b.** sweeter　**c.** more sweet ) than dark chocolate.

2. Airplanes fly ( **a.** higher than　**b.** more high　**c.** more higher than ) helicopters.

3. Al is tall, but Bob is ( **a.** tallest　**b.** taller than　**c.** the tallest ) boy in the class.

4. The book was ( **a.** interesting more than　**b.** more interesting than　**c.** more than interesting ) the movie.

5. Lucy drives ( **a.** carefully　**b.** more careful　**c.** more carefully ) than Greg.

6. This is the ( **a.** worst　**b.** worse　**c.** most badly ) weather we've had all spring.

7. Martin arrived the ( **a.** earlier　**b.** most early　**c.** earliest ) to the party.

8. Of all my friends, Beth speaks ( **a.** the most honestly　**b.** more honestly　**c.** the most honest ).

 **Reading Helper**

日本語の意味に合うように、下の￼から適切な語句を選び、正しい形に変えて英文を完成させましょう。マーカーを引いた語句は次ページの **Reading Challenger** に出てくる重要語句です。

| bad | busy | careful | delicious | good | healthy | long | low |

1. Jo does many tasks in the office. He's the ＿＿＿＿＿ and ＿＿＿＿＿ worker.
（ジョーはオフィスで多くの仕事をこなしています。彼は最も忙しくて、最も注意深い従業員です）

2. Is Jake a ＿＿＿＿＿ soccer player than you? –Yes. In fact, I'm the ＿＿＿＿＿ player on the team.　（ジェイクはあなたよりもサッカーが上手ですか。—はい。実際、私はチームでいちばん下手な選手です）

3. Pizza is ＿＿＿＿＿ than salad. On the other hand, salad is ＿＿＿＿＿.
（ピザはサラダよりも美味しいです。その一方でサラダはより健康的です）

4. In Japan, "black" companies are untrustworthy. They also have ＿＿＿＿＿ working hours than other companies, and they offer the ＿＿＿＿＿ pay.
（日本ではブラック企業は信用できません。またそれらは他の企業よりも就業時間が長く、最も給料が低いです）

## Reading Challenger

**A** （　　　）内のa、bから適切な語句を選び、英文を完成させましょう。その後で音声を聞いて答えを確認しましょう。　　**CheckLink**　🎧 DL 49　◎ CD 49

In today's digital age, managing daily tasks like banking, shopping and making reservations has never been easier. However, there are some problems with these types of online activities. First, doing tasks online is [1]( **a.** safer  **b.** riskier ) than doing them in person or by phone. In fact, online identity theft is now the most
5　[2]( **a.** common  **b.** unusual ) way of stealing personal information.

Second, online sites give limited information and guidance to customers. Person-to-person interactions, on the other hand, are more [3]( **a.** helpful  **b.** careless ) and [4]( **a.** negative  **b.** effective ) in dealing with customers' questions or concerns.

Third, many websites are untrustworthy. It's sometimes hard to know the
10　difference between a genuine website and a fake one. This presents a [5]( **a.** higher **b.** lower ) risk of online scams, such as internet shoppers unknowingly making payments to scammers.

Finally, one of the most [6]( **a.** similar  **b.** serious ) concerns about doing tasks online is the risk of people losing their ability to communicate effectively with
15　others on a personal level. Creating a good balance between the convenience of the digital age and the value of genuine human connections is necessary.

**◖NOTES◗**

identity theft「個人情報詐取」  limited「限られた」  genuine「本物の」  scams「詐欺」
unknowingly「知らないうちに」  scammers「詐欺師」

**B** 英文の内容に合うようにa～dを並べかえ、サマリーを完成させましょう。

CheckLink

**a** The risk of losing one's ability to interact well with others is a major problem with doing tasks online. It's important to have a balanced approach to technology and personal connections.

**b** Without knowing, many people lose money by paying for things on fake websites.

**c** Face-to-face interactions provide customers with better guidance than the limited information available on online sites.

**d** Doing daily tasks online is convenient. However, there are risks, such as online identity theft.

1. ☐ ➡ 2. ☐ ➡ 3. ☐ ➡ 4. ☐

**C** 英文の内容を正しく述べている文になるよう、a、bから適切な語句を選びましょう。

CheckLink

1. Doing tasks by phone is ( **a.** riskier  **b.** safer ) than doing tasks online.

2. ( **a.** Online sites  **b.** Human workers ) are more effective in answering customer's questions.

3. ( **a.** Scammers unknowingly make payments to customers.  **b.** Customers unknowingly make payments to scammers. )

4. The passage suggests that ( **a.** most people have lost their ability to communicate with others  **b.** the digital age is convenient, but comes with risks ).

# Useful Words & Phrases

**A** 右の▇から適切な語句を選びフレーズを完成させましょう。その後で音声を聞いて答えを確認しましょう。　🎧 DL 50　💿 CD 50

1. ............................ and receive email
2. ............................ an online map
3. ............................ for information
4. ............................ a movie
5. ............................ a photo with friends
6. ............................ with friends

chat
search
send
share
stream
use

**B** a～f のイラストに合うフレーズを **A** の1～6から選び（　　）に書きましょう。

a. (　　　)

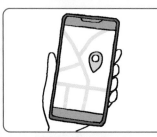

b. (　　　)

c. (　　　)

d. (　　　)

e. (　　　)

f. (　　　)

**C** 下の▇から適切な語句を選び英文を完成させましょう。その後で音声を聞いて答えを確認しましょう。　🎧 DL 51　💿 CD 51

chat　complete　discuss　read　search　share　stream

For me, the internet is my most valuable tool. For entertainment, I often
¹............................ movies and music. I also ²............................ with friends a lot. It's fun
to ³............................ their text messages and ⁴............................ various topics. We often
⁵............................ photos, too. And as a university student, I regularly ⁶............................ for
information on the internet. It helps me to ⁷............................ my assignments.

**NOTE** assignments「課題」

70

# Getting Around in the Future

未来時制

POINT!!

- will と be going to の使い分け
- 未来時制の否定文と疑問文の形

## Reading Starter

CheckLink  DL 52  CD 52

英文を読み、話の流れに合うようにa～dの
イラストを並べましょう。

How will people travel in the future?
Here are some predictions. Our roads are
going to be filled with eco-friendly electric
cars, mostly self-driving. Hi-speed trains
5 and hyperloop systems will conveniently
connect distant cities. Hoverboards, like
in the movie *Back to the Future*, aren't
going to appear anytime soon, though.
Traditional ways of traveling, such as
10 by train and airplane, won't disappear.
They will continue to connect cities
and countries around the world. And
to maintain good health, walking and
cycling are going to remain an important
15 part of our lives.

**NOTES**

predictions「予測」 eco-friendly「環境にやさしい」
hyperloop「ハイパーループ (真空状態のチューブの中で
列車を高速移動させる構想中のシステム)」 distant「遠く
離れた」 hoverboards「ホバーボード (空中に浮いて移動
するスケートボードに似た乗り物。SF の世界で用いられる)」

1. ☐ ⇒ 2. ☐ ⇒ 3. ☐ ⇒ 4. ☐

# Grammar Review

will と be going to は未来のことについて言うときに使います。状況によってどちらも使用できる場合もありますが、一方しか使えない場合もあります。

① 未来の予測や起こりそうなことについて話す ➡ will または be going to

It **will** rain later today. / It **is going** to rain later today.

② その場で決めたこれから行う行動について話す ➡ will

A: We don't have any bread.  B: OK, I **will** go to the store and buy some.

③ 未来のいつか必ず起こると分かっていることについて話す ➡ will

In the future, everyone **will** use robots.

④ あらかじめ決めていた未来の予定や意図について話す ➡ be going to

I **am going to** play tennis with Carl on Sunday.

⑤ 兆候や理由があって、確実にすぐ起こることについて話す ➡ be going to

I didn't charge my phone last night.  It **is going to** die soon.

---

**will**　willの後ろに動詞の原形を続けます。

▶ 形と語順

| 主語 | 肯定文 | 否定文 | 疑問文 |
|---|---|---|---|
| I / you / he / she / it / we / they | I **will** ['ll] be [go, play, practice] | I **will not** [won't] be [go, play, practice] | **Will** you be [go, play, practice] …? |

It **will be** hot today. / It **won't be** hot today. / **Will** it **be** hot today?

---

**be going to**　going toの後ろに動詞の原形を続けます。be動詞は主語によって変わります。

▶ 形と語順

| 主語 | 肯定文 | 否定文 | 疑問文 |
|---|---|---|---|
| I | I **am** ['m] **going to** be [go, play, practice] | I **am not** ['m not] **going to** be [go, play, practice] | **Am** I **going to** be [go, play, practice] …? |
| you / we / they | you **are** ['re] **going to** be [go, play, practice] | you **are not** [aren't] **going to** be [go, play, practice] | **Are** you **going to** be [go, play, practice] …? |
| he / she / it | he **is** ['s] **going to** be [go, play, practice] | he **is not** [isn't] **going to** be [go, play, practice] | **Is** he **going to** be [go, play, practice] …? |

It**'s going to be** hot today. / It **isn't going to be** hot today. / **Is** it **going to be** hot today?

**Grammar Check-Up**

**A** もう一度**Reading Starter**の英文を読み、未来形〈will ＋動詞の原形〉と〈be going to ＋動詞の原形〉に下線を引きましょう。全部で７か所見つけられますか。

**B** （　　　）内のa〜cから適切な語句を選び、英文を完成させましょう。その後で音声を聞いて答えを確認しましょう。　CheckLink　DL 53　CD 53

1. ( **a.** I'm going　**b.** I'll　**c.** I will to ) clean my room this afternoon.

2. Glen ( **a.** isn't going to　**b.** won't going to　**c.** is going to not ) sell his guitar.

3. ( **a.** I'll　**b.** I'm going　**c.** I'll to ) help you clean the house tomorrow.

4. ( **a.** Will start you　**b.** Are you going start　**c.** Will you start ) work soon?

5. The ball ( **a.** going　**b.** will　**c.** is going ) to hit the car.

6. ( **a.** Will you　**b.** Are you　**c.** You'll ) going to watch the game on TV?

7. Annie ( **a.** won't be　**b.** will be not　**c.** isn't going to ) home for dinner.

8. Where ( **a.** you're going　**b.** will you　**c.** are you going ) to go camping?

## Reading Helper

日本語の意味に合うように、下の　　から適切な語句を選び英文を完成させましょう。
マーカーを引いた語句は次ページの**Reading Challenger** に出てくる重要語句です。

| add | finish | improve | know | receive | send | take | tell |
|-----|--------|---------|------|---------|------|------|------|

1. I'm going to ＿＿＿＿＿ the goods today.  You'll ＿＿＿＿ them tomorrow.
   （今日品物を送る予定です。それらは明日届きます）

2. Our public transportation will ＿＿＿＿＿ next year.  The city is going to ＿＿＿＿＿ more buses and routes.
   （当社の公共交通機関は来年改善される予定です。その都市にはより多くのバスの便と路線が加わります）

3. Thanks to everyone's efforts, we're going to ＿＿＿＿＿ the project on time.  I'll ＿＿＿＿＿ Mr. Brown the good news.
   （皆さんのご尽力のおかげで私たちはそのプロジェクトを予定どおりに終わらせることができそうです。私はその良い知らせをブラウンさんに伝えます）

4. Who's going to replace Fred on the sales team?  —It's going to ＿＿＿＿＿ several weeks to find someone.  We won't ＿＿＿＿＿ until next month.
   （誰がフレッドの代わりに販売チームに加わりますか。―誰か (代わりの人) を見つけるのに数週間かかりそうです。私たちには来月になるまでわかりません）

## Reading Challenger

**A** （　　　）内のa、bから適切な語句を選び、英文を完成させましょう。その後で音声を聞いて答えを確認しましょう。　　CheckLink　　DL 54　　CD 54

A hyperloop is a system of capsules that carries people or goods through low-pressure tubes. Recently, hyperloops have received much attention as the next major form of transportation. Hyperloop systems will [1]( **a.** travel **b.** break ) at speeds of more than 1,100 kilometers per hour. This is going to greatly
5　[2]( **a.** increase **b.** reduce ) travel times between cities.

Building hyperloop systems [3]( **a.** will **b.** will not ) come with a high price tag, and tickets will likely be expensive for the first several years. However, thanks to the efficient design of hyperloops, ticket prices will slowly [4]( **a.** rise and fall **b.** fall and become ) more affordable for a wider range of people.

10　Hyperloops will run on electric energy, using only renewable energy such as solar and wind power to make electricity. With their clean energy, hyperloop systems will [5]( **a.** have **b.** take ) a great impact on promoting more eco-friendly modes of transportation.

Hyperloops [6]( **a.** are going to **b.** are not going to ) replace trains, buses and
15　airplanes. However, many experts predict that they will become the next big thing in transportation, changing the way people move from one place to another.

**NOTES**

capsules「カプセル」 tubes「チューブ、管」 efficient「効率のよい」 affordable「（値段が）手頃な」
electric「電気の」 renewable energy「再生可能エネルギー」 electricity「電気」

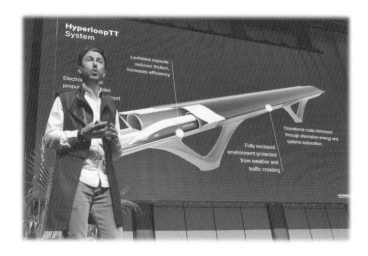

**B** 英文の内容に合うようにa～dを並べかえ、サマリーを完成させましょう。

CheckLink

**a** Hyperloops will use clean energy and promote "green" transportation.

**b** The cost of building hyperloops will be high. Riding them will also be expensive at first, with ticket prices becoming more reasonable over time.

**c** Hyperloops won't replace traditional forms of transportation, but they'll probably become a common way for people to travel in the future.

**d** Hyperloops are a new type of high-speed transportation system using capsules and tubes.

1. ☐ ➡ 2. ☐ ➡ 3. ☐ ➡ 4. ☐

**C** 英文の内容を正しく述べている文になるよう、a、bから適切な語句を選びましょう。

CheckLink

1. Hyperloops use ( **a.** low-pressure    **b.** high-pressure ) tubes.

2. The hyperloop ( **a.** design is efficient    **b.** designers are efficient ).

3. Hyperloop systems will operate using ( **a.** natural gas    **b.** electric power ).

4. Experts predict that hyperloops will ( **a.** replace traditional trains    **b.** become a popular form of transportation ) in the future.

# Useful Words & Phrases

**A** 右の　　から適切な語句を選びフレーズを完成させましょう。その後で音声を
聞いて答えを確認しましょう。　🎧 DL 55　💿 CD 55

1. use a delivery _____
2. drive a flying _____
3. ride an electric _____
4. wear jet-powered _____
5. travel through time in a time _____
6. be in a traffic _____

| boots |
| car |
| drone |
| jam |
| machine |
| scooter |

**B** a～f のイラストに合うフレーズを **A** の１～６から選び（　　）に書きましょう。

a. (　　　)　　　　b. (　　　)　　　　c. (　　　)

d. (　　　)　　　　e. (　　　)　　　　f. (　　　)

**C** 下の　　から適切な語句を選び英文を完成させましょう。その後で音声を聞いて
答えを確認しましょう。　🎧 DL 56　💿 CD 56

| bird　boots　cars　jams　reality　roads　transportation |

In the future, I believe we'll have ultra-fast and convenient public ¹_____
– and there will be no more traffic ²_____. I think flying ³_____ will be
a common sight, too. Maybe we won't need ⁴_____ anymore. As for me, I
dream of wearing jet-powered ⁵_____ and flying like a ⁶_____. Do you
think my dream will become a ⁷_____?

# Virtual Reality Is Really Here

助動詞

POINT!!

● 助動詞の種類とそれぞれの意味

● 助動詞を使った否定文と疑問文の形

## Reading Starter

CheckLink    DL 57    CD 57

英文を読み、話の流れに合うようにa～dの
イラストを並べましょう。

Virtual reality (VR) allows you to explore
different worlds – and you don't have to
leave your home to do it!  By wearing a
headset, you can do almost anything,
5  like walking on the Moon or going on
a thrilling safari.  VR hand controllers
allow you to touch objects and perform
different types of actions.  You might
reach out and grab a virtual basketball
10  and shoot it into a virtual basket.  Or you
may want to touch a playful dolphin as
you experience an exciting underwater
adventure.  The possibilities for VR are
"virtually" endless.

**NOTES**

explore「…を探検する」 grab「…をつかむ」
dolphin「イルカ」 virtually「ほとんど」
endless「無限の」

1. ☐ ➡ 2. ☐ ➡ 3. ☐ ➡ 4. ☐

# Grammar Review

助動詞は、「能力」「許可」「依頼」「可能性」などの意味を動詞に付け加えるときに使います。
助動詞の後ろには動詞の原形が続きます。

> Janet **can play** the piano. (ジャネットはピアノを弾くことができます)

## 助動詞の種類

| 機能 | 助動詞 | 例文 |
|---|---|---|
| 能力 | **can** (…できる)<br>**could** (…できた) | I **can** swim.<br>(私は泳ぐことができます) |
| 許可 | **may / can / could**<br>(…してもいい) | **May** I leave early today?<br>(今日早退してもいいですか) |
| 依頼 | **can / could / will / would**<br>(…してもらえますか) | **Could** you help me?<br>(手伝っていただけませんか) |
| 可能性 | **may / might / could**<br>(…かもしれない) | It **might** snow tomorrow.<br>(明日雪が降るかもしれません) |
| アドバイス | **should / ought to / had better**<br>(…したほうがいい、…すべき) | You **should** take a rest.<br>(休息したほうがいい) |
| 義務・必要性 | **must / have to**<br>(…しなければならない) | I **have to** leave now.<br>(今、出発しなければなりません) |
| 禁止 | **cannot / must not**<br>(…してはいけない) | You **cannot** eat here.<br>(ここで食べることはできません) |
| 確実性 | **must** (…にちがいない)<br>**cannot** (…であるはずがない) | The store **must** be closed.<br>(お店は閉まっているにちがいない) |

**助動詞の否定文**：助動詞の後ろに **not** を置いて動詞の原形を続けます。**have to** の場合は **don't [doesn't]** や **didn't** を **have to** の前に置きます。

| | | |
|---|---|---|
| can→ **cannot [can't]** | could→ **could not [couldn't]** | may→ **may not** |
| will→ **will not [won't]** | would→ **would not [wouldn't]** | might→ **might not** |
| should→ **should not [shouldn't]** | ought to→ **ought not to** | had better→ **had better not** |
| must→ **must not [mustn't]** | have to→ **don't [doesn't] have to** | |

Bob **can't** ski. / I **don't have to** study.

**助動詞の疑問文**：助動詞を主語の前に出します。**have to** の場合は **do [does]** や **did** を主語の前に置きます。

**Can** Bob ski? / **Do** I **have to** study?

## Grammar Check-Up

**A** もう一度 **Reading Starter** の英文を読み、助動詞に下線を引きましょう。全部で4か所見つけられますか。

**B** （　　　）内のa～cから適切な語句を選び、英文を完成させましょう。その後で音声を聞いて答えを確認しましょう。　CheckLink　DL 58　CD 58

1. Yuta can ( **a.** speak　**b.** to speak　**c.** speaking ) English very well.

2. ( **a.** May　**b.** Should　**c.** Would ) you pass the salt, please?

3. Take your umbrella.  It ( **a.** had better　**b.** must　**c.** might ) rain later.

4. ( **a.** May borrow I　**b.** I may borrow　**c.** May I borrow ) your eraser?

5. This pie is delicious.  You ( **a.** should　**b.** ought　**c.** had better ) to have some.

6. Do you ( **a.** have to　**b.** must　**c.** may ) take classes on Saturdays?

7. That ( **a.** ought not　**b.** can't　**c.** doesn't have to ) be Tim.  He's out of town.

8. We ( **a.** might no　**b.** don't have to　**c.** mustn't ) wear jeans to work.  It's a rule.

## Reading Helper

日本語の意味に合うように、下の□□から適切な語句を選び英文を完成させましょう。
マーカーを引いた語句は次ページの **Reading Challenger** に出てくる重要語句です。

| can't　couldn't　had to　have to　might　should　shouldn't　would |
| --- |

1. We _____ leave our barbecue tools outside. _____ you put them in the garage?
   （私たちはバーベキューの道具を外に放置すべきでありません。それらをガレージの中にしまってもらえますか）

2. We _____ visit the historical site this morning.  We _____ wait until the afternoon.
   （今朝私たちはその史跡を訪れることができませんでした。私たちは午後まで待たなければなりませんでした）

3. What foreign language _____ I study?  I _____ decide.
   （どの外国語を私は勉強すべきでしょうか。私は決められません）

4. I _____ boost my attendance in this class or I _____ fail.
   （私はこの授業の出席数を増やさなければなりません。さもないと単位を落とすかもしれません）

**Reading Challenger**

**A** （　　　）内のa、bから適切な語句を選び、英文を完成させましょう。その後で
音声を聞いて答えを確認しましょう。　CheckLink　🎧DL 59　◎CD 59

These days, many universities are using virtual reality (VR) as an educational tool. VR gives students the opportunity to easily visit and interact with places and objects. For instance, they [1]( **a.** can　**b.** must ) experience exciting adventures by exploring historical sites, or by taking an amazing journey deep inside the human
5　body.

In addition, by participating in virtual conversations, students' foreign-language speaking and listening abilities [2]( **a.** can't　**b.** may ) improve. Interacting with virtual characters, or avatars, [3]( **a.** might　**b.** had to ) also boost their confidence and motivate them to study harder.

10　In regular classrooms, students [4]( **a.** had better not　**b.** may not ) always receive the necessary help from their teachers. But with VR, students can learn at their own pace and focus on their needs. They [5]( **a.** don't have to　**b.** must not ) follow the same approach as others or listen to explanations about things they already understand.

15　In summary, virtual reality can make learning more exciting and effective for students. However, VR [6]( **a.** has to　**b.** shouldn't ) replace traditional classrooms. Combining VR with traditional teaching methods is an effective way to maximize student learning.

**NOTES**

in addition「さらに、加えて」 avatars「アバター」 approach「取り組み方法」 in summary「要約すれば」
methods「方法」 maximize「…を最大にする」

**B** 英文の内容に合うようにa〜dを並べかえ、サマリーを完成させましょう。

CheckLink

**a** With virtual reality, students can focus on their own learning needs, without following others or receiving instruction about things they already know.

**b** Many universities now use virtual reality for education, allowing students to explore places and objects easily.

**c** The best way for students to learn is by combining virtual reality with traditional teaching methods.

**d** Virtual reality can help students learn another language and encourage them to study more.

**1.** ☐ ➡ **2.** ☐ ➡ **3.** ☐ ➡ **4.** ☐

**C** 英文の内容を正しく述べている文になるよう、a、bから適切な語句を選びましょう。

CheckLink

**1.** Using VR, students can ( **a.** visit places from the past　**b.** design virtual reality games ).

**2.** VR allows students to have conversations with ( **a.** real native speakers **b.** virtual language partners ) of other languages.

**3.** Teachers ( **a.** don't always　**b.** never ) have time to meet the needs of every student.

**4.** The passage suggests that ( **a.** VR classrooms are better than traditional classrooms　**b.** classrooms can work effectively using both traditional teaching methods and VR technology ).

# Useful Words & Phrases

**A** 右の ■■■ から適切な語句を選びフレーズを完成させましょう。その後で音声を
聞いて答えを確認しましょう。　　　　　　🎧 DL 60　◎ CD 60

1. attend a virtual _____

2. create a virtual _____

3. do virtual _____

4. play a virtual _____

5. ride a virtual theme park _____

6. try on virtual _____

> attraction
> make-up
> painting
> party
> sport
> training

**B** a〜f のイラストに合うフレーズを **A** の 1〜6 から選び（　　）に書きましょう。

a. (　　　)　　　　　　b. (　　　)　　　　　　c. (　　　)

d. (　　　)　　　　　　e. (　　　)　　　　　　f. (　　　)

**C** 下の ■■■ から適切な語句を選び英文を完成させましょう。その後で音声を聞いて
答えを確認しましょう。　　　　　　🎧 DL 61　◎ CD 61

> attractions　countries　experiences　lines　museums　paintings　sports

Virtual reality is a great way to enjoy unique [1]_____. I can ride virtual
theme park [2]_____ without leaving my home – and I don't have to wait in
long [3]_____. I can also play virtual [4]_____ like tennis or soccer. As
an art student, it's really exciting to be able to visit famous virtual [5]_____ in
different [6]_____. I can also create virtual [7]_____.

# Unit

# 13
# Pet Adoption

## 接続詞

POINT!!
● 接続詞の役割
● 等位接続詞と従属接続詞の使い方

## 📖 Reading Starter

↻ CheckLink  🎧 DL 62  ◎ CD 62

英文を読み、話の流れに合うようにa～dの
イラストを並べましょう。

Japanese people love keeping pets, so
it's only natural that pet shops are
popular places.  Pet shops in Japan sell
a variety of animals, including dogs,
5 cats, rabbits, birds and fish.  Most shops
also provide products such as pet food
and toys.  Some shops offer services
such as grooming and training, too.
Although you can still find pets for sale
10 in the United States, England and other
Western countries, most pet shops today
offer only pet supplies and services.
This shift has happened because most
people nowadays prefer adopting pets
15 from animal shelters instead of buying
them.

**NOTES**

grooming「グルーミング（被毛のブラッシングや爪切りな
どペットの手入れ）」 Western countries「西洋諸国」
nowadays「近頃」 adopting「…（動物）を引き取ること」
animal shelters「動物保護施設」

1. ⬜ ➡ 2. ⬜ ➡ 3. ⬜ ➡ 4. ⬜

# Grammar Review

接続詞とは単語や句、文同士をつなぐために使われる語です。

Tom **and** Cathy are good friends.（トムとキャシーは良い友達です）

I check my mail **before** I go to bed.（私は寝る前にメールをチェックします）

| 等位接続詞 | 単語と単語、句と句、文と文をつなぎます。 |
| --- | --- |

| | | | |
| --- | --- | --- | --- |
| **and**「そして、…と～」 | | **but**「しかし、だが」 | |
| 単語： | It's cool **and** windy today. | 単語： | The class is long **but** interesting. |
| 句： | He gets up **and** has breakfast. | 句： | He likes to drive, **but** not at night. |
| 文： | She talked **and** I listened. | 文： | I was tired, **but** I couldn't sleep. |
| **or**「…または～」 | | **so**「それで、だから」 | |
| 単語： | Do you want tea now **or** later? | 文： | Jack overslept, **so** he was late for class. |
| 句： | Is Don at home **or** at the store? | | |
| 文： | We can study **or** we can relax. | ※soは文と文のみをつなぎます。 | |

| 従属接続詞 | 文と文をつなぎます。時や理由、条件などを示します。 |
| --- | --- |

| | |
| --- | --- |
| **before**「…する前に」<br>Set your alarm **before** you go to bed.<br>（寝る前にアラームをセットしなさい） | **when**「…するとき」<br>I'll call **when** I reach the station.<br>（駅に着いたら電話します） |
| **after**「…する後に」<br>What will you do **after** you graduate?<br>（卒業した後、あなたは何をしますか） | **while**「…している間に」<br>I read **while** I'm on the train.<br>（私は電車に乗っているときに本を読みます） |
| **because**「…なので」<br>I'm happy **because** I passed the test.<br>（私はテストに合格したので幸せです） | **if**「もし…なら」<br>Let me know **if** you need help.<br>（助けが必要なら知らせてください） |
| **although**「…だけれども」<br>The house is nice **although** it's small.<br>（その家は小さいけれど素敵です） | **unless**「もし…でないなら」<br>I'll play golf **unless** it rains.<br>（雨が降らなければ、私はゴルフをします） |

※従属接続詞に続く部分は、文の前半に置くこともできます。その場合、接続詞に続く部分の
終わりにコンマ (,) をつけます。

Set your alarm **before** you go to bed. = **Before** you go to bed, set your alarm.

## Grammar Check-Up

**A** もう一度**Reading Starter**の英文を読み、等位接続詞には<u>下線</u>を、従属接続詞には波線を引きましょう。全部で8か所見つけられますか。

**B** (　　　)内のa〜cから適切な語句を選び、英文を完成させましょう。その後で音声を聞いて答えを確認しましょう。　⟳CheckLink 🎧DL 63 ◎CD 63

**1.** The music was loud ( **a.** but　**b.** or　**c.** so ) enjoyable.

**2.** I lost my phone, ( **a.** after　**b.** because　**c.** so ) I can't text my friends.

**3.** ( **a.** After　**b.** Unless　**c.** While ) the party ended, we cleaned up the house.

**4.** Don't touch the fruit ( **a.** and　**b.** after　**c.** unless ) you're going to buy it.

**5.** You shouldn't drive ( **a.** although　**b.** but　**c.** when ) you're tired.

**6.** ( **a.** Before　**b.** If　**c.** While ) we leave now, we can catch the next train.

**7.** I can't meet you tonight ( **a.** although　**b.** because　**c.** before ) I have to work.

**8.** ( **a.** Although　**b.** If　**c.** So ) it rained every day, we had fun in London.


## Reading Helper

日本語の意味に合うように、下の□□□から適切な語句を選び英文を完成させましょう。マーカーを引いた語句は次ページの**Reading Challenger**に出てくる重要語句です。

| although | and | but | if | or | so | unless | when |
|----------|-----|-----|-----|-----|-----|--------|------|

**1.** ＿＿＿＿＿ my job is very challenging, it is also enjoyable ＿＿＿＿＿ satisfying.
（私の仕事はとてもやりがいがありますが、また楽しいし満足感を得られます）

**2.** Jerry is a firefighter, ＿＿＿＿＿ he sometimes rescues people.  He feels joy ＿＿＿＿＿ he is able to save lives.
（ジェリーは消防士なのでときどき人々を救助します。命を救うことができたとき、彼は喜びを感じます）

**3.** ＿＿＿＿＿ Ken's treatment is successful, he can leave the hospital in two ＿＿＿＿＿ three days.
（ケンの治療が成功すれば、彼は2日か3日後に退院することができます）

**4.** Professor Jones has a friendly ＿＿＿＿＿ quiet personality.  He doesn't usually talk ＿＿＿＿＿ he has something important to say.
（ジョーンズ教授は友好的ですが無口な性格です。何か話すべき重要なことがなければ彼はふだん話しません）

**A** ( ) 内のa、bから適切な語句を選び、英文を完成させましょう。その後で
音声を聞いて答えを確認しましょう。　　　CheckLink 🎧 DL 64 ◎ CD 64

[1]( **a.** When　**b.** While ) Americans get pets, they usually adopt them from
animal shelters instead of buying them from pet shops. Adopting a pet can be very
satisfying [2]( **a.** because　**b.** unless ) it provides a loving home for animals in need.
It also gives the animals a second chance at life.

5　　People adopt pets for various reasons. Some people just want to save an
animal's life. Others prefer not to support pet breeding, knowing that there are
so many homeless animals in shelters. Adopting a pet can also be much more
affordable than buying from a breeder [3]( **a.** and　**b.** or ) a pet shop.

　　Animal shelters rescue and care for animals, and help them [4]( **a.** although　**b.** if )
10　they require medical treatment. They also organize adoption events [5]( **a.** and
**b.** but ) educate people about the benefits and responsibilities of adopting.

　　[6]( **a.** Before　**b.** After ) a person adopts a pet, shelters give them information
about the animal's personality, health and suitability for young children. Thanks
to the hard work of shelters across the United States, millions of animals have
15　found good homes through pet adoption.

**NOTES**

breeding「繁殖、品種改良」 breeder「ブリーダー」 organize「…(行事など) を企画 [準備] する」
benefits「利点」 suitability「適合性」

86

**B** 英文の内容に合うようにa～dを並べかえ、サマリーを完成させましょう。

CheckLink

**a** Shelters help people to choose the right pet by providing information about the animals. They have successfully placed millions of animals in good homes.

**b** Instead of buying pets from pet shops, Americans usually get them from shelters. This provides animals with good homes and an opportunity for a better life.

**c** Animal shelters rescue, care for and provide medical assistance for animals. They also hold events and give people important information about pet adoption.

**d** Reasons for adopting a pet include saving an animal, choosing not to support pet breeding and saving money.

1. ☐ ➡ 2. ☐ ➡ 3. ☐ ➡ 4. ☐

**C** 英文の内容を正しく述べている文になるよう、a、bから適切な語句を選びましょう。

CheckLink

1. It is ( a. common   b. uncommon ) for Americans to buy pets from pet shops.

2. Pet adoption is ( a. cheaper than   b. more expensive than ) buying from a pet shop.

3. At events, animal shelters ( a. look for volunteer workers   b. tell visitors about the merits of pet adoption ).

4. Shelters provide information about the ( a. character   b. history ) of the animals.

# Useful Words & Phrases

**A** 右の⬚から適切な語句を選びフレーズを完成させましょう。その後で音声を聞いて答えを確認しましょう。

🎧 DL 65　◎ CD 65

1. clean your pet's living _____
2. join a pet training _____
3. take your pet for a _____
4. teach your pet a _____
5. get a _____
6. visit a pet _____

area
café
class
trick
vaccine
walk

**B** a〜f のイラストに合うフレーズを **A** の1〜6から選び（　　）に書きましょう。

a. (　　　)

b. (　　　)

c. (　　　)

d. (　　　)

e. (　　　)

f. (　　　)

**C** 下の⬚から適切な語句を選び英文を完成させましょう。その後で音声を聞いて答えを確認しましょう。

🎧 DL 66　◎ CD 66

air　　café　　home　　meal　　shelter　　tricks　　walk

A few months ago, my wife and I adopted our dog Candy from an animal
[1] _____. Every day, we take her for a [2] _____ in the park for some fresh
[3] _____ and exercise. When we're at [4] _____, my wife likes to teach
her [5] _____ like "shake hands" and "roll over." Sometimes we visit a pet
[6] _____. There, Candy can meet other dogs and eat a special [7] _____.

88

# Unit 14

# Mobile Supermarkets to the Rescue

受動態

**POINT!!**
- 受動態（現在形・過去形）の作り方
- 受動態の否定文と疑問文の形

## 📖 Reading Starter

↻ CheckLink 🎧 DL 67 ◎ CD 67

英文を読み、話の流れに合うようにa～dの
イラストを並べましょう。

In urban areas of Japan, a wide range
of shopping options are offered – from
department stores and shopping malls,
to supermarkets and convenience stores.
5 These areas are served by excellent
public transportation systems, allowing
easy access. However, as more people
move to cities, populations in rural areas
have decreased and many stores have
10 closed. Many bus and train services
have also stopped. This has resulted in
a serious problem for elderly residents –
"food deserts." The term is often used
to describe areas with limited access to
15 fresh and affordable food.

**NOTES**

urban「都市［都会］の」
served by ...「（地域などに）…が普及した」
rural「田舎の」　result in ...「（結果的に）…をもたらす」
residents「住民」　deserts「砂漠」

1. ☐ ➡ 2. ☐ ➡ 3. ☐ ➡ 4. ☐

受動態は、「…される、…された」という意味を表します。しばしば、動作を行う人・物が不明な場合や明白で述べる必要のない場合に使用されます。また、動作を行う人・物よりも、動作を受ける人・物や動作そのものが重要な場合に使用されます。

能動態　Cleaners clean the floors every day. （清掃員が毎日床を掃除します）

受動態　The floors are cleaned every day. （床は毎日掃除されます）

## 受動態の形と語順

肯定文　〈主語＋be動詞＋過去分詞〉

| |
|---|
| I am ['m]＋過去分詞　I'm paid [grown, made] … |
| you [we, they]＋are ['re]＋過去分詞　They're paid [grown, made] … |
| he [she, it]＋is ['s]＋過去分詞　She's paid [grown, made] … |
| I [he, she, it]＋was＋過去分詞　I was paid [grown, made] … |
| you [we, they]＋were＋過去分詞　They were paid [grown, made] … |

I'm paid $15 an hour. / Peas are grown here. / The house is made of wood.
I was paid $15 an hour. / Peas were grown here. / The house was made of wood.

否定文　〈主語＋be動詞＋not＋過去分詞〉

| |
|---|
| I am not ['m not]＋過去分詞　I'm not paid [grown, made] … |
| you [we, they]＋are not [aren't]＋過去分詞　They aren't paid [grown, made] … |
| he [she, it]＋is not [isn't]＋過去分詞　He isn't paid [grown, made] … |
| I [he, she, it]＋was not [wasn't]＋過去分詞　I wasn't paid [grown, made] … |
| you [we, they]＋were not [weren't]＋過去分詞　They weren't paid [grown, made] … |

I'm not paid $15 an hour. / Peas aren't grown here. / The house isn't made of wood.
I wasn't paid $15 an hour. / Peas weren't grown here. / The house wasn't made of wood.

疑問文　〈be動詞＋主語＋過去分詞 …?〉

| |
|---|
| Am I＋過去分詞 …?　Am I paid [grown, made] …? |
| Are you [we, they]＋過去分詞 …?　Are they paid [grown, made] …? |
| Is he [she, it]＋過去分詞 …?　Is he paid [grown, made] …? |
| Was I [he, she, it]＋過去分詞 …?　Was I paid [grown, made] …? |
| Were you [we, they]＋過去分詞 …?　Were they paid [grown, made] …? |

Am I paid $15 an hour? / Are peas grown here? / Is the house made of wood?
Was I paid $15 an hour? / Were peas grown here? / Was the house made of wood?

## Grammar Check-Up

**A** もう一度 **Reading Starter** の英文を読み、受動態〈be動詞＋過去分詞〉に下線を引きましょう。全部で3か所見つけられますか。

**B** (　　　) 内のa～cから適切な語句を選び、英文を完成させましょう。その後で音声を聞いて答えを確認しましょう。　CheckLink　DL 68　CD 68

1. The door ( **a.** is locking　**b.** has locked　**c.** is locked ) at night.

2. My newspaper ( **a.** wasn't　**b.** isn't　**c.** hasn't ) delivered this morning.

3. Are ( **a.** sold shoes　**b.** shoes sale　**c.** shoes sold ) at this store?

4. Students ( **a.** don't allow　**b.** aren't allowed　**c.** not allowed ) to eat in class.

5. These houses ( **a.** built　**b.** are built　**c.** were built ) 100 years ago.

6. Is ( **a.** French spoken　**b.** speaking French　**c.** French speaking ) in Canada?

7. This ring ( **a.** has given　**b.** was given　**c.** were given ) to me by my mother.

8. Where ( **a.** these pictures were taken　**b.** were taken these pictures　**c.** were these pictures taken )?

## Reading Helper

日本語の意味に合うように、下の◻️から適切な語句を選び、受動態に変えて英文を完成させましょう（疑問文の場合もあります）。マーカーを引いた語句は次ページの **Reading Challenger** に出てくる重要語句です。

| announce | attend | call | change | hold | make | tell | use |

1. A free concert ＿＿＿＿＿ in the park yesterday. According to the news, it ＿＿＿＿＿ by more than 20,000 people.　（昨日無料コンサートが公園で開かれました。ニュースによれば、2万人以上の人がそれに参加しました）

2. These snacks ＿＿＿＿＿ YumBars. They ＿＿＿＿＿ with dried fruit and chocolate.　（これらのおやつはヤムバーと呼ばれています。それらはドライフルーツとチョコレートで作られています）

3. ＿＿＿＿＿ you ＿＿＿＿＿ in advance about the meeting? –No, it ＿＿＿＿＿ just ＿＿＿＿＿.
（あなたは前もって会議について伝えられていましたか。—いいえ、たった今知らされました）

4. Every year, the bus route ＿＿＿＿＿ because a street on the route ＿＿＿＿＿ for a parade.　（ルート上の通りがパレードに使われるので、毎年そのバスのルートは変更されます）

**A** (　　　) 内のa、bから適切な語句を選び、英文を完成させましょう。その後で
音声を聞いて答えを確認しましょう。　　　ⒸCheckLink　🎧DL 69　◎CD 69

Mobile supermarkets were ¹( **a.** held　**b.** introduced ) in Japan in the 1970s.
They were first ²( **a.** designed　**b.** entered ) to bring food and other daily necessities
to small communities without nearby stores.　Today, they have become essential
lifelines for thousands of elderly people across rural Japan.

5　　The operators of mobile supermarkets usually follow a schedule.　The routes
are ³( **a.** needed　**b.** planned ) according to the needs and location of people in
the various areas.　Schedules are ⁴( **a.** given　**b.** received ) to the communities in
advance, so residents can prepare for the arrival of the trucks.

A large number of food items are ⁵( **a.** paid　**b.** sold ) from the food trucks.　They
10　include fresh fruits and vegetables, milk and eggs, meat and fish, rice, canned
goods and snacks.　Other items such as cleaning and healthcare products are also
available for sale.

Mobile supermarkets not only provide an essential service for the elderly.
They also serve as a convenient meeting place for neighbors to interact and share
15　information.　It is ⁶( **a.** feared　**b.** hoped ) that traveling stores will continue to
support elderly residents in rural communities for many years in the future.

---

**⟨NOTES⟩**

mobile supermarkets「移動スーパー」　daily necessities「日用品」　essential「必要不可欠な」
lifelines「命綱、頼みの綱」　canned goods「缶詰製品」　neighbors「近所の人々」

**B** 英文の内容に合うようにa～dを並べかえ、サマリーを完成させましょう。

CheckLink

**a** Mobile supermarkets operate on schedules and carefully planned routes, enabling shoppers to prepare in advance for their arrival.

**b** Mobile supermarkets have become very important for Japan's elderly population in rural areas.

**c** Mobile supermarkets bring food to rural communities. They are also an important gathering place for elderly people to talk and exchange information.

**d** Mobile supermarkets sell a wide variety of food items and other daily products.

**1.** ☐ ➡ **2.** ☐ ➡ **3.** ☐ ➡ **4.** ☐

**C** 英文の内容を正しく述べている文になるよう、a、bから適切な語句を選びましょう。

CheckLink

**1.** In the 1970s, mobile supermarkets were brought to ( **a.** small  **b.** large ) communities.

**2.** Food truck shoppers can ( **a.** pay for food items  **b.** receive schedules ) in advance.

**3.** Mobile supermarkets sell ( **a.** personal care items  **b.** only fresh food ).

**4.** It is hoped that mobile supermarkets ( **a.** will not be needed  **b.** will keep helping elderly people ) in rural areas in the future.

# Useful Words & Phrases

**A** 右の ▓▓ から適切な語句を選びフレーズを完成させましょう。その後で音声を聞いて答えを確認しましょう。　🎧 DL 70　◎ CD 70

1. travel to a rural _____
2. purchase products from a local _____
3. sample _____
4. provide home food _____
5. offer a _____
6. accept an online _____

> delivery
> discount
> farmer
> food
> order
> town

**B** a〜f のイラストに合うフレーズを **A** の 1〜6 から選び（　）に書きましょう。

a. (　　)　　　　b. (　　)　　　　c. (　　)

d. (　　)　　　　e. (　　)　　　　f. (　　)

**C** 下の ▓▓ から適切な語句を選び、必要に応じて形を変えて英文を完成させましょう。その後で音声を聞いて答えを確認しましょう。　🎧 DL 71　◎ CD 71

> accept　operate　provide　purchase　sell　support　travel

Toshi was born and raised in a small town in Japan. Now he ¹_____ a mobile supermarket. He ²_____ to small towns and ³_____ food and other daily items. He often ⁴_____ products from local farmers. He also ⁵_____ home food delivery for some of his elderly customers and ⁶_____ online orders. Toshi happily ⁷_____ rural Japanese communities.

**NOTE** raised「育てられて」

## Unit 15

# Time Performance

関係詞

POINT!!
- 関係詞の役割
- 関係詞の種類と使い分け

### Reading Starter

CheckLink   DL 72   CD 72

英文を読み、話の流れに合うようにa～dの
イラストを並べましょう。

Many Japanese Gen Z (Gen Z-ers), or
people who were born between the mid-
1990s and early 2010s, place importance
on time performance, or *taipa* as they call
5  it.  They live in a time when efficiency
and punctuality are highly valued. Here
are some situations where *taipa* is
maximized:

■ Not participating in an after-work
10   dinner party that has no purpose

■ Watching a video at double the normal
speed

■ Preparing a meal which can be eaten
over a period of several days

15 ■ Doing a small task during a television
commercial break

**NOTES**

Gen Z (Generation Z) 「Z世代」  efficiency 「効率」
punctuality 「時間厳守」  valued 「評価された」
purpose 「目的」

1. ☐ ➡ 2. ☐ ➡ 3. ☐ ➡ 4. ☐

95

# Grammar Review

関係詞とは、文中の名詞を説明する文を付け加えるために使用される語です。

The man is a baker. **He lives next door.** ➡ The man **who** lives next door is a baker.
（男性はパン屋さんです。彼は隣に住んでいます。➡ 隣に住んでいる男性はパン屋さんです）

The umbrella is mine. **You took it.** ➡ The umbrella **that** you took is mine.
（その傘は私のです。あなたがそれを取りました。➡ あなたが取った傘は私のです）

## 関係詞の種類

文中で使用する関係詞の種類は、文の中での役割に応じて決まります。

| 関係詞 | 説明する名詞 | 例文 |
|---|---|---|
| who | 人 | The woman **who** helped me was kind.<br>（私を助けてくれた女性は親切でした） |
| that | 物 | The chocolate **that** you like comes from Belgium.<br>（あなたが好きなチョコレートはベルギー産です） |
| | 人 | That's the person **that** found my wallet.<br>（あれが私の財布を見つけてくれた人です） |
| which | 物 | That's the café **which** serves the best cheesecake.<br>（あれが最高のチーズケーキを出すカフェです） |
| whose | 人 | The child **whose** toy broke cried.<br>（おもちゃが壊れた子どもは泣きました） |
| | 物 | The plant **whose** leaves are yellow needs water.<br>（葉っぱが黄色い植物は水を必要としています） |
| where | 場所 | The hotel **where** we stayed was excellent.<br>（私たちが泊まったホテルは素晴らしかったです） |
| when | 時 | He enjoyed the time **when** he lived in the U.S.<br>（彼はアメリカに住んでいた時期を楽しみました） |
| why | 理由 | Tell me the reason **why** you chose this university.<br>（あなたがこの大学を選んだ理由を教えてください） |

## 関係詞の省略

who、that、whichは文中で目的語の役割を担っている場合、しばしば省略されます。

My friend lives in L.A. **I visited** him. ➡ My friend (**who** [**that**]) **I visited** lives in L.A.
This phone is very light. **I bought** it. ➡ This phone (**that** [**which**]) **I bought** is very light.

96

**Grammar Check-Up**

**A** もう一度 **Reading Starter** の英文を読み、関係詞に下線を引きましょう。全部で5か所見つけられますか。

**B** （　　　）内の a ～ c から適切な語句を選び、英文を完成させましょう。その後で音声を聞いて答えを確認しましょう。　↻ CheckLink　🎧 DL 73　◎ CD 73

1. The person ( **a.** who　**b.** whose　**c.** which ) won the contest is my best friend.

2. Dan works for a company ( **a.** where　**b.** which　**c.** whose ) makes windows.

3. We went to a quiet place ( **a.** that　**b.** who　**c.** where ) we could talk.

4. Did you find the book ( **a.** where　**b.** that　**c.** who ) you were looking for?

5. I don't know the reason ( **a.** that　**b.** which　**c.** why ) Sam quit his job.

6. An artist ( **a.** which　**b.** that　**c.** why ) I really like is Picasso.

7. Spring is a time ( **a.** when　**b.** why　**c.** whose ) families often take vacations.

8. I always shop at stores ( **a.** who　**b.** that　**c.** whose ) prices are reasonable.


**Reading Helper**

日本語の意味に合うように、下の　　から適切な語句を選び英文を完成させましょう。
マーカーを引いた語句は次ページの **Reading Challenger** に出てくる重要語句です。

| when | where | which | who | who | whose | whose | why |
| --- | --- | --- | --- | --- | --- | --- | --- |

1. The Louvre is a museum ＿＿＿＿＿＿ many valuable artworks are displayed.
   The painting ＿＿＿＿＿ most people come to see is the *Mona Lisa*.
   (ルーブル美術館は多くの貴重な芸術作品が展示されている美術館です。ほとんどの人が観にくる絵画はモナ・リザです)

2. Lynn is a dancer ＿＿＿＿＿ techniques are excellent, but there are days
   ＿＿＿＿＿ her energy level is low.
   (リンは技術の素晴らしいダンサーですが、元気のない日があります)

3. Jane is a responsible friend ＿＿＿＿＿ I met in high school. She only buys
   clothes ＿＿＿＿＿ production methods are eco-friendly.　(ジェーンは私が高校で出会った信頼できる友達です。彼女は製造方法が環境にやさしい衣服しか買いません)

4. Ben is the only worker ＿＿＿＿＿ has a light workload. I can't understand the
   reason ＿＿＿＿＿ his manager allows that.　(ベンは作業負荷の軽い唯一の従業員です。私はマネージャーがそれを許している理由が理解できません)

**Reading Challenger**

**A** ( ) 内のa、bから適切な語句を選び、英文を完成させましょう。その後で
音声を聞いて答えを確認しましょう。　 CheckLink 　DL 74　 CD 74

The lives of many university students are filled with classes, homework, club activities, part-time jobs, and so on.  This busy lifestyle is the reason [1]( **a.** where **b.** why ) time performance is so valuable to them.  Students [2]( **a.** who **b.** whose ) focus on important tasks and manage their time effectively are more likely to
5　reach their goals and achieve personal growth.

Good time performance requires techniques [3]( **a.** that **b.** who ) improve students' productivity.  They include planning ahead and dividing large tasks into smaller parts.  These strategies help students reduce stress and achieve more success in their studies and other activities.

10　Punctuality is another area of time performance [4]( **a.** why **b.** which ) is very important for university students.  Being punctual not only shows that students are reliable and responsible, but also considerate of other people's time.

Finally, in group projects, time performance is maximized during periods [5]( **a.** why **b.** when ) the workload is evenly divided among team members.  This
15　motivates individual members to work hard and successfully complete their tasks.  It also creates a positive and productive environment [6]( **a.** where **b.** who ) everyone's efforts are valued.

**NOTES**

productivity「生産性」 strategies「戦略、方策（単数形：strategy）」 punctual「時間を守る」
considerate「思いやりのある」 periods「期間」 evenly divided「均等に分けられた」

**B** 英文の内容に合うようにa～dを並べかえ、サマリーを完成させましょう。

CheckLink

**a** During group work, good time performance is achieved by dividing tasks equally and working hard together toward a common goal.

**b** Being on time is very important for university students. It has a positive impact on their time performance and shows respect for other people's time.

**c** Good time management techniques enable students to be more productive, feel less stress and succeed in their classes and other areas.

**d** Busy university students value time performance. It helps them to balance classes and other activities, to meet their goals and to grow as individuals.

1. ☐ ➡ 2. ☐ ➡ 3. ☐ ➡ 4. ☐

**C** 英文の内容を正しく述べている文になるよう、a、bから適切な語句を選びましょう。

CheckLink

1. The passage suggests that students ( a. have busy schedules    b. do not manage their time effectively ).

2. By dividing one large task into several smaller tasks, students' stress levels ( a. increase    b. decrease ).

3. Punctuality plays a ( a. major    b. minor ) part in time performance.

4. Group projects are most successful when ( a. there are several group leaders b. each member feels that their work is valued ).

# Useful Words & Phrases

**A** 右の ▨ から適切な語句を選びフレーズを完成させましょう。その後で音声を聞いて答えを確認しましょう。
🎧 DL 75  💿 CD 75

1. _____ a checklist
2. _____ three healthy meals a day
3. _____ organized
4. _____ your phone
5. _____ in a quiet place
6. _____ a time limit

be
eat
make
put away
set
study

**B** a〜f のイラストに合うフレーズを **A** の1〜6から選び（　　）に書きましょう。

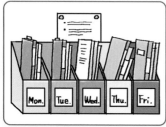

**a. (　　)**

**b. (　　)**

**c. (　　)**

**d. (　　)**

**e. (　　)**

**f. (　　)**

**C** 下の ▨ から適切な語句を選び英文を完成させましょう。その後で音声を聞いて答えを確認しましょう。
🎧 DL 76  💿 CD 76

eat　　enjoy　　follow　　give　　improve　　make　　put away

To make the best use of my time, I ¹_____ a few simple strategies. First, I ²_____ a checklist of tasks that I need to do each day. Second, I ³_____ my phone before studying so I can stay focused. Lastly, for maximum energy, I ⁴_____three healthy meals a day. These strategies ⁵_____ my time performance and ⁶_____ me more time to ⁷_____ my hobbies.

このシールをはがすと
**CheckLink** 利用のための
**「教科書固有番号」**が
記載されています。

一度はがすと元に戻すことは
できませんのでご注意下さい。

4188 Reading Leader

◀ ここからはがして下さい

CheckLink

---

本書には CD（別売）があります

---

# Reading Leader

基本文法から始める初級リーディング

2024 年 1 月 20 日　初版第 1 刷発行
2024 年 2 月 20 日　初版第 2 刷発行

著　者　Robert Hickling

発行者　福　岡　正　人

発行所　株式会社　金星堂

（〒 101-0051）東京都千代田区神田神保町 3-21
Tel. (03) 3263-3828（営業部）
(03) 3263-3997（編集部）
Fax (03) 3263-0716
https://www.kinsei-do.co.jp

編集担当　戸田浩平　　　　　　　　　　　Printed in Japan
印刷所・製本所／三美印刷株式会社

ISBN978-4-7647-4188-1　C1082